THE BEST OF
JIMMIE VAUGHAN

Music transcriptions by John Garwood, Jesse Gress and Andrew Moore
Cover photo by Robert Knight / Retna

ISBN 0-634-07945-X

HAL•LEONARD®
CORPORATION

7777 W. BLUEMOUND RD. P.O. BOX 13819 MILWAUKEE, WI 53213

Visit Hal Leonard Online at
www.halleonard.com

from Jimmie Vaughan - *Strange Pleasure*

Boom-Bapa-Boom

Written by Jimmie Vaughan

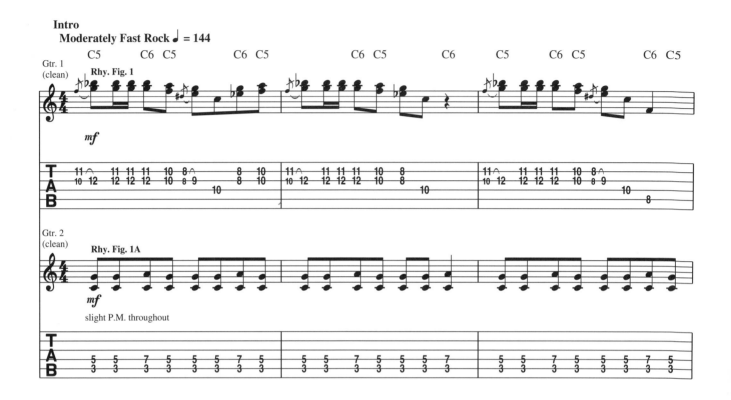

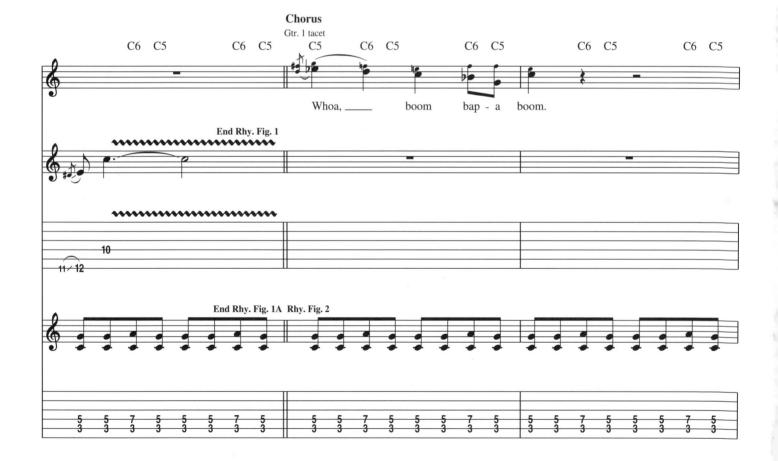

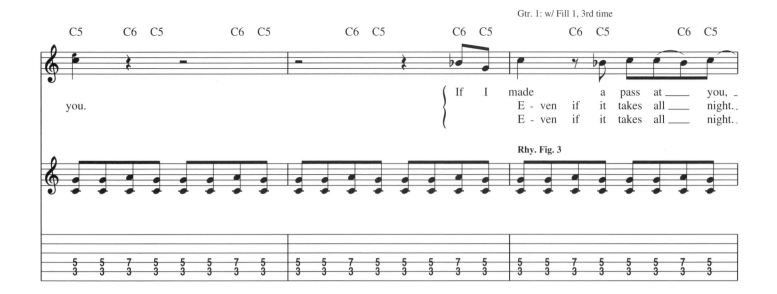

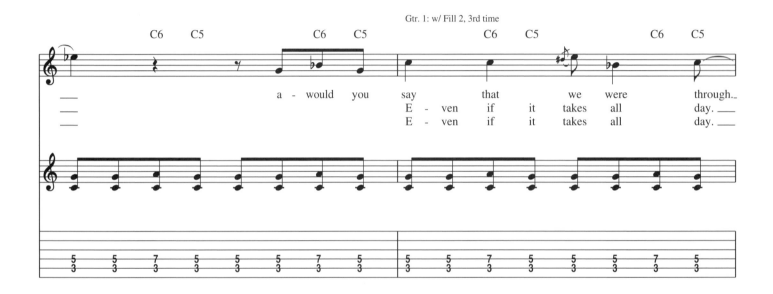

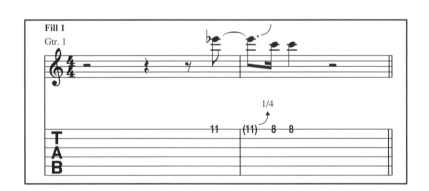

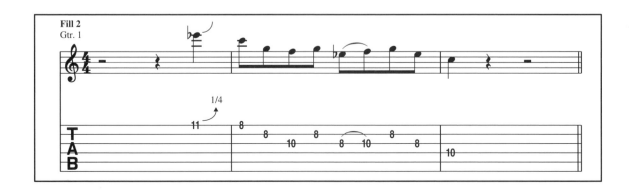

Guitar Solo

Gtr. 2: w/ Rhy. Fig. 3, 2 times

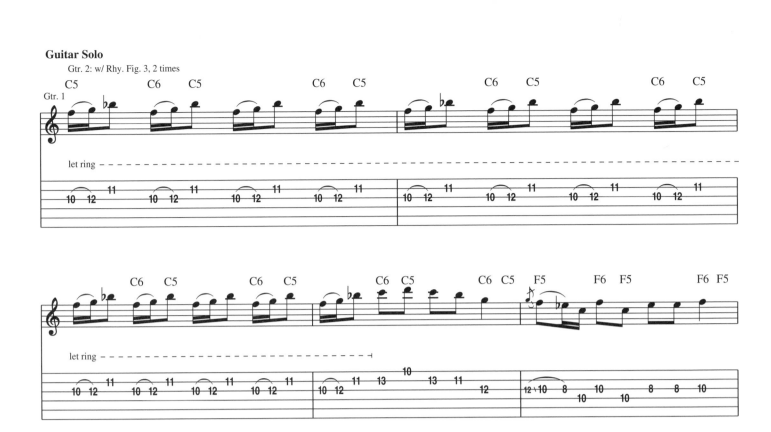

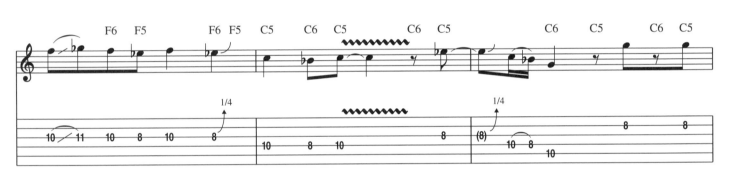

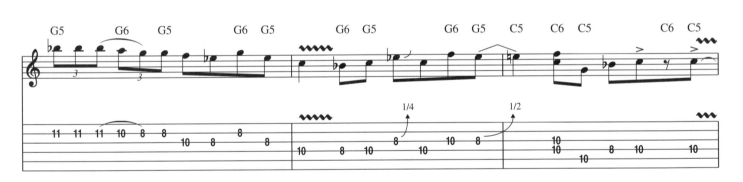

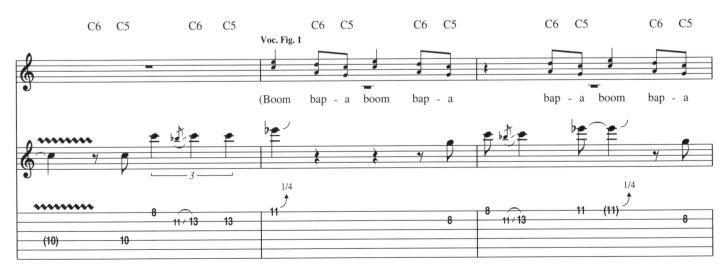

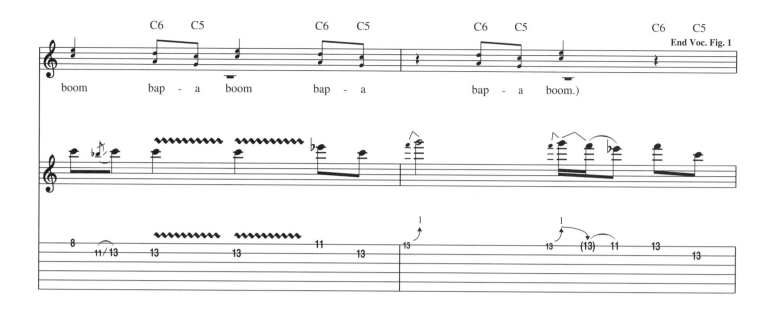

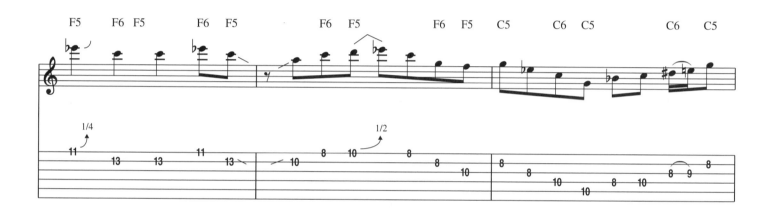

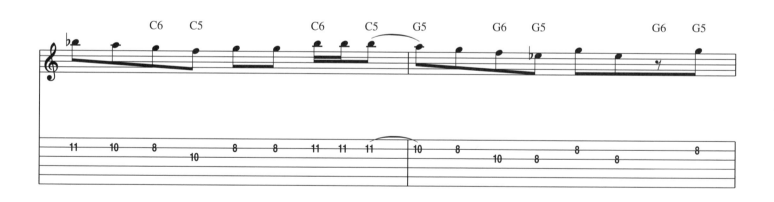

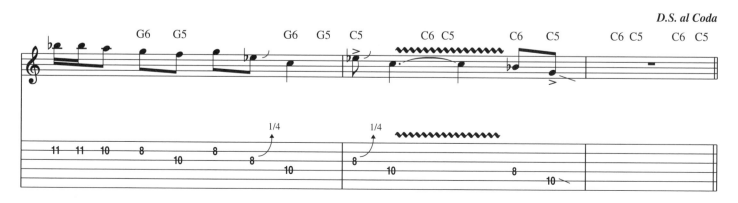

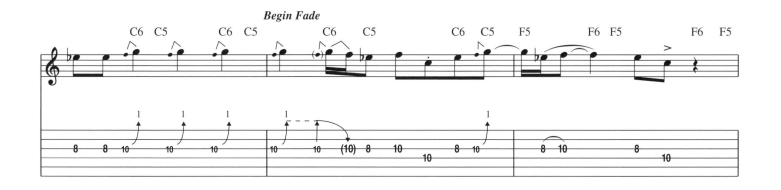

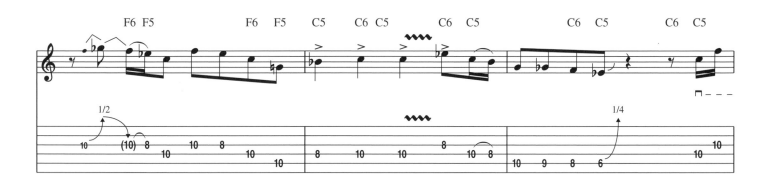

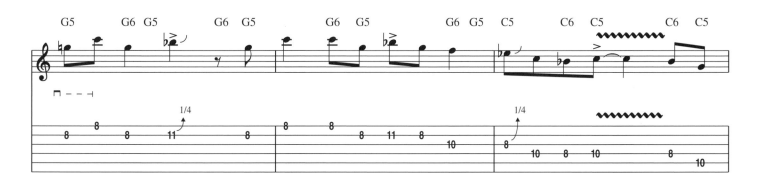

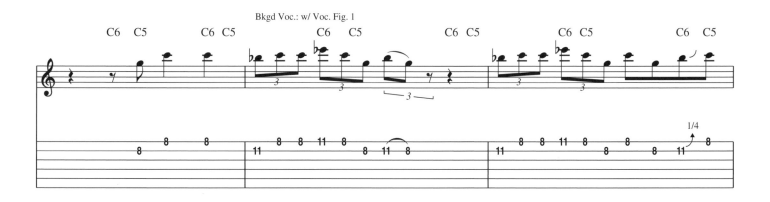

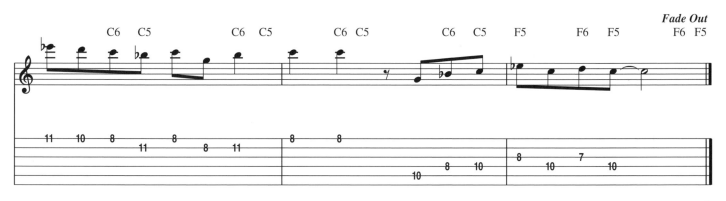

from Jimmie Vaughan - *Out There*

Can't Say No

Written by Jimmie Vaughan

Capo IV

Intro
Moderate Blues ♩. = 77

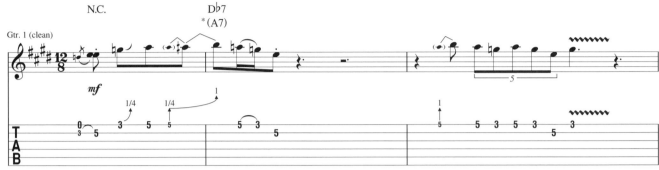

*Symbols in parentheses represent chord names respective to capoed guitar.
Symbols above reflect actual sounding chords. Capoed fret is "0" in tab.
Chord symbols reflect overall harmony.

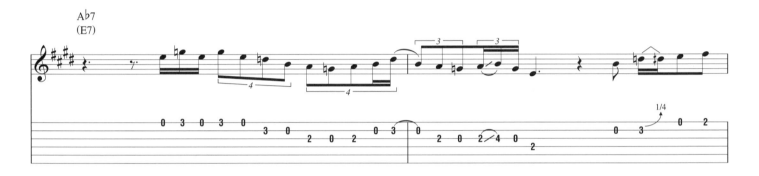

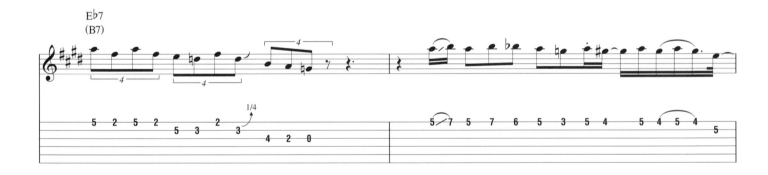

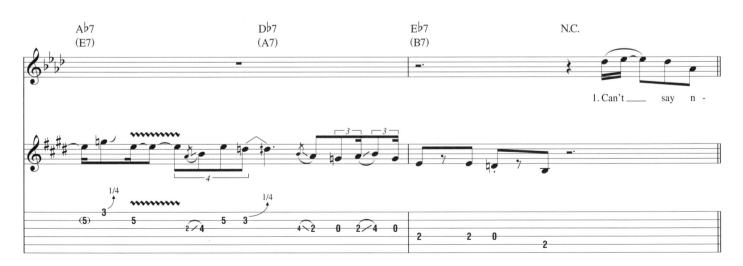

1. Can't ___ say n-

*Refers to upstemmed voc. only.

**As before.

D.S. al Coda

$\bigoplus$ **Coda**

from The Vaughan Brothers-*Family Style*

Good Texan

Written by Jimmie Vaughan and Nile Rodgers

You look ro - man - tic lay - in'
Rid - in' the range ___ I
Mas - sive ward - robe of

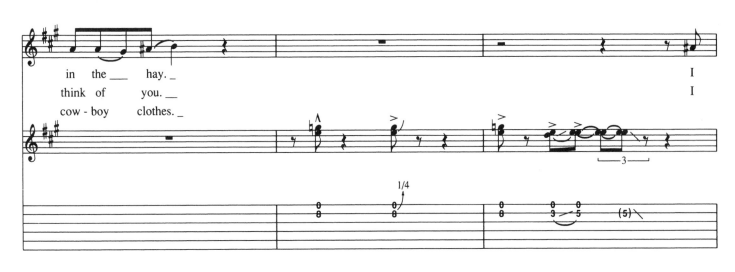

in the ___ hay. _ I
think of you. _ I
cow - boy clothes. _

need ya to - night _ in a new kind of way. _
dig your chil - i, you know it's true. _____
Top of my head to the tip of my toes. _

* Cue notes on 2nd, 3rd verses

18

When _ ya look at ____ me, __ ah, with those _ eyes, _____
Aw, I make big mon - ey, put it in the bank. _____
Aw, you look so good in my hat with fringe on it.

3rd time, Gtr. 2: w/ Fill 1

it makes me start __ to fan-
That long - horn Cad - dy's got a
So put on my boots mmm _

Fill 1
Gtr. 2

ta - size. _____
great big tank. _____
dog - gone it. ___

Do it   to __ me like I   know you _ could, _ so I can   do it   to you ba - by like a   Tex - an __ should. _

say you need a fel-la who real-ly ___ can, ___ do it to you good like a

Tex - an man. _____

(Ha, ha, ha, ha, ha, ha, ha!)

Guitar solo

Mmm. _____

straight ♪'s ---- ┐   straight ♪'s ---- ┐

(J.V.)

*Rhy. Fig. 3

* Rhy. Fig. 3 includes acous. gtr. part.

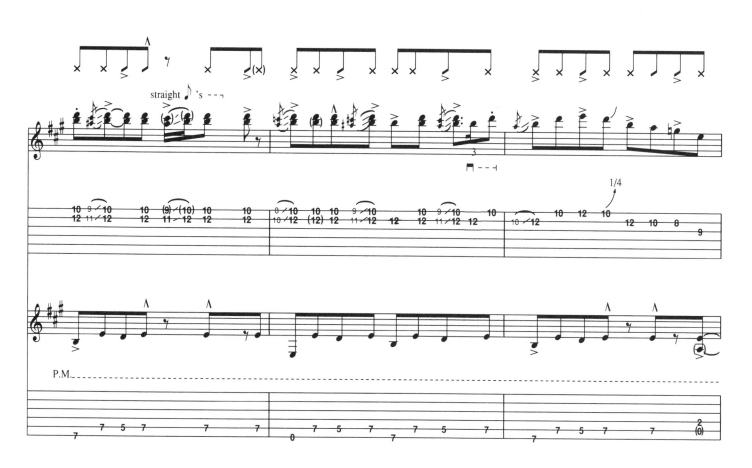

straight ♪'s --- ┐

1/4

P.M.--

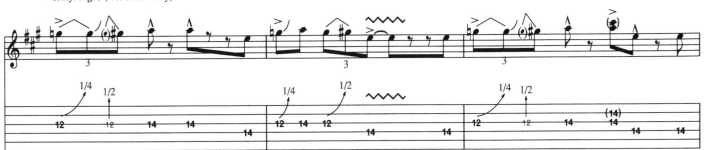

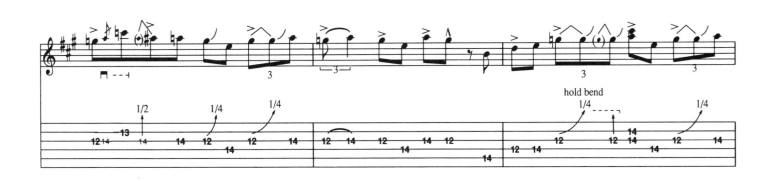

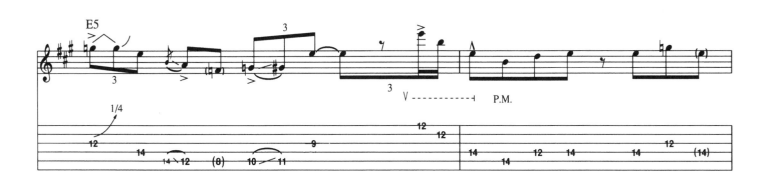

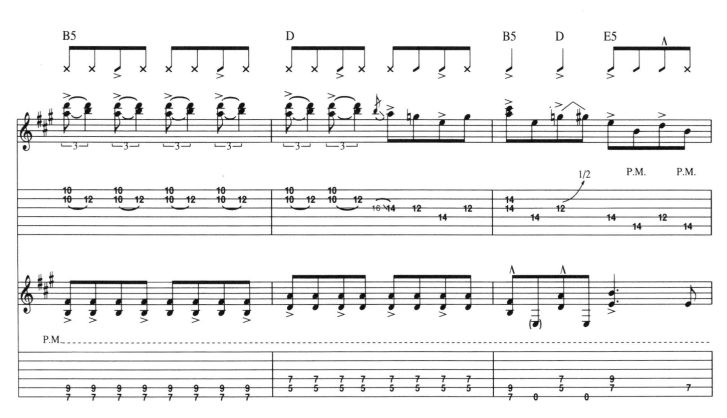

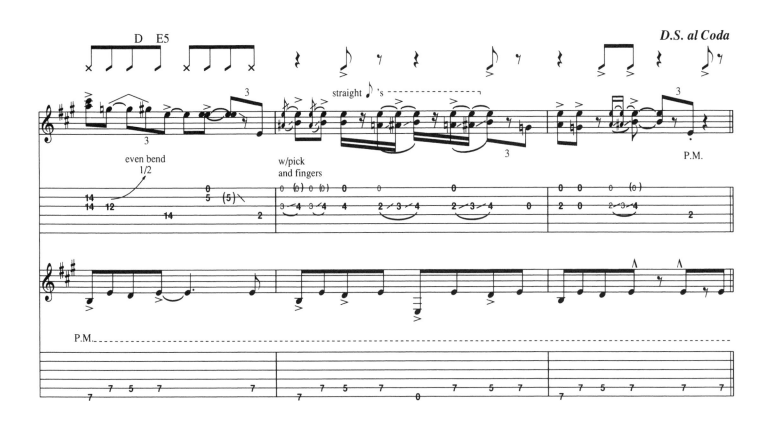

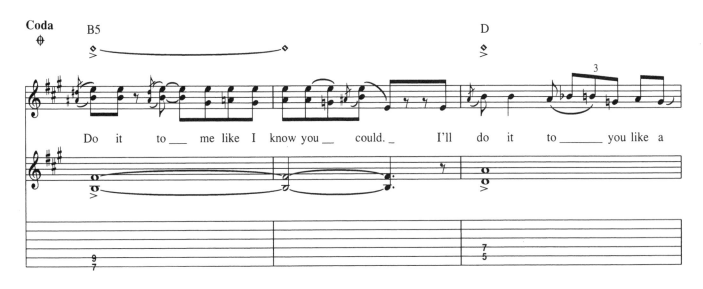

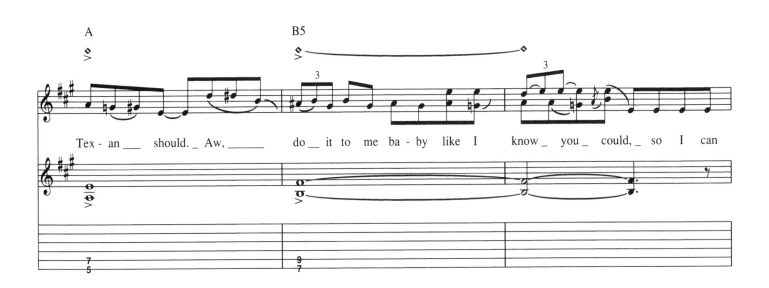

do it to ya ba - by like a Tex - an ____ should. ____

Oh, _____

mmm. _____

(Spoken:) That's right ba - by, c' mere and ri - ri - ride that po - ny a - cross this

bridge! You're a good ___

from Jimmie Vaughan - *Strange Pleasure*

Just Like Putty

Written by Jimmie Vaughan and Paul Henry Ray

Gtr. 1; Capo III

Intro

Moderately Slow Blues ♩. = 76

* Piano & bass arr. for gtr.

** Symbols in parentheses represent chord names respective to capoed gtr. Symbols above reflect actual sounding chords. Capoed fret is "0" in tab.

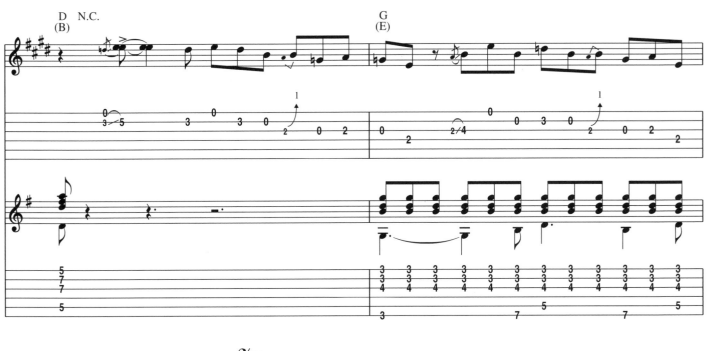

%Verse

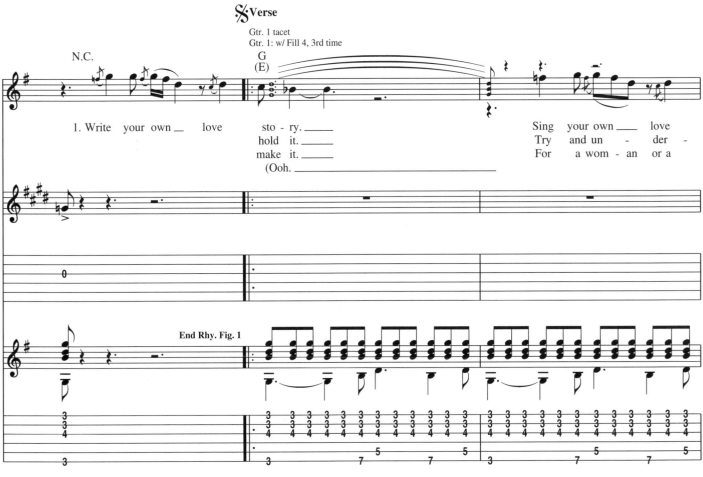

Gtr. 1 tacet
Gtr. 1: w/ Fill 4, 3rd time

1. Write your own ___ love sto- ry. ___
hold it. ___
make it. ___
(Ooh. ___

Sing your own ___ love
Try and un- der-
For a wom- an or a

End Rhy. Fig. 1

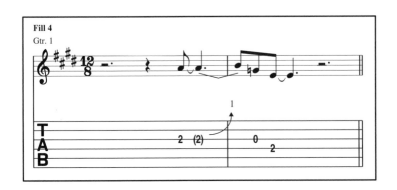

Fill 4
Gtr. 1

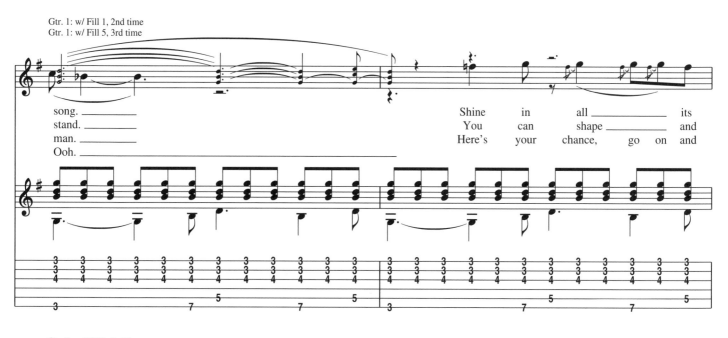

song. _____   Shine   in   all _____ its
stand. _____   You   can   shape ____ and
man. _____   Here's   your   chance,   go   on   and
Ooh. _____

To Coda 1

C7
(A7)

A7   N.C.
(F♯7)

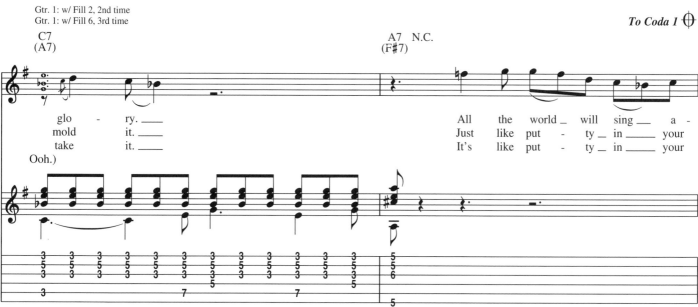

glo -   ry. ____   All   the   world _ will   sing _ a -
mold   it. ____   Just   like   put - ty _ in ___ your
take   it. ____   It's   like   put - ty _ in ___ your
Ooh.)

Fill 1
Gtr. 1

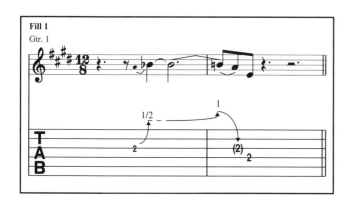

Fill 2
Gtr. 1

Fill 5
Gtr. 1

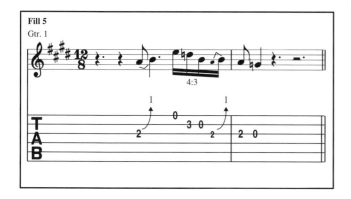

Fill 6
Gtr. 1

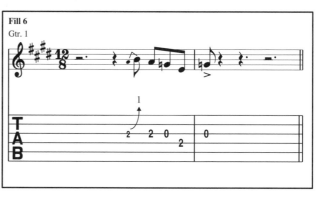

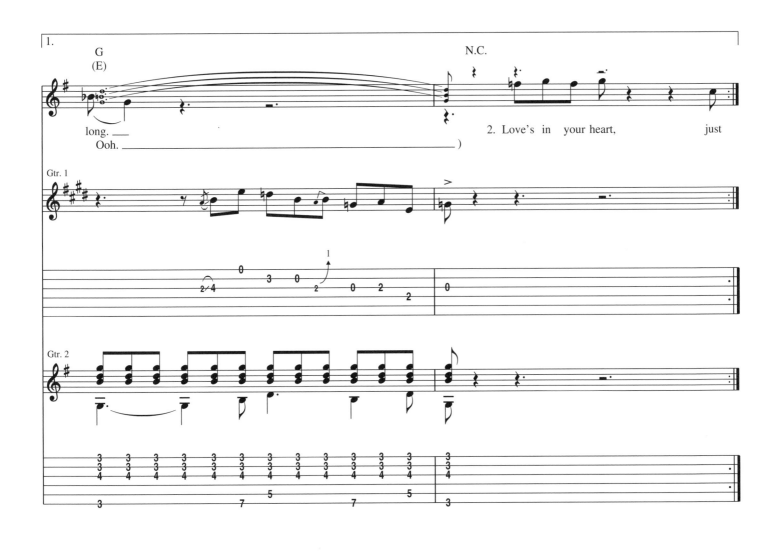

1.

long. ___

Ooh. ___

2. Love's in your heart,   just

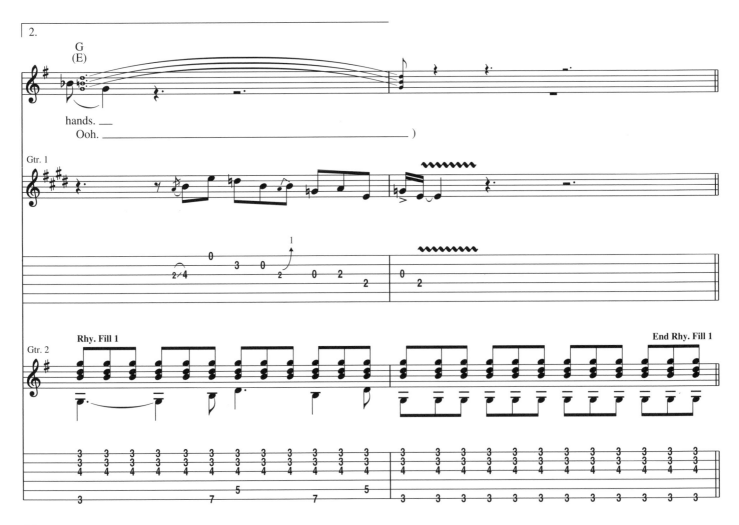

2.

hands. ___

Ooh. ___

you   will have a   love su - preme.

you will have ___ a love that lasts.

from Jimmie Vaughan - *Out There*

Like a King

Words and Music by Nile Rodgers

Gtr. 2: Capo III

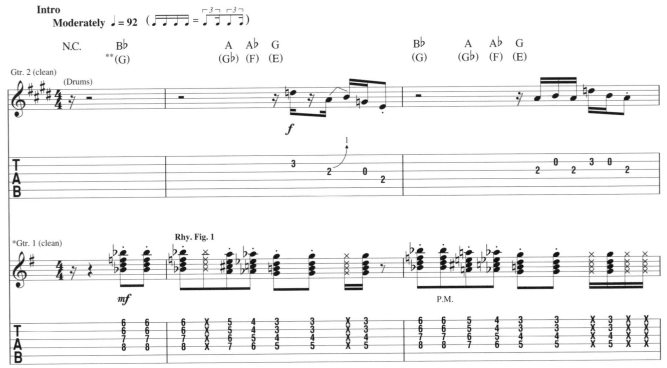

*Two gtrs. arr. for one. **Symbols in parentheses represent chord names respective to capoed guitar.
Symbols above reflect actual sounding chords. Capoed fret is "0" in tab.

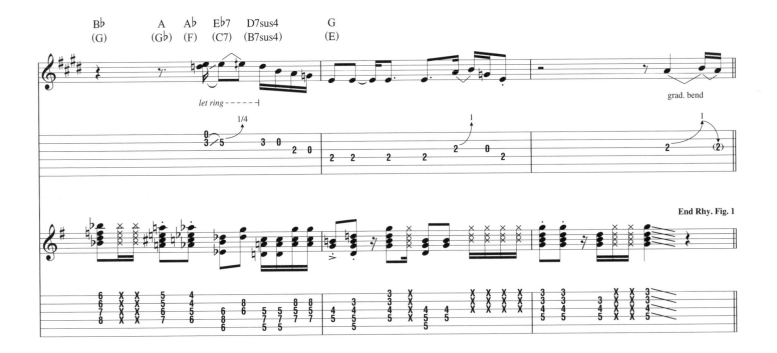

Voice that sounds like birds in the spring._____ She make me

Chorus

feel ____ like a king, ____

feel ____ like a king, ____

feel ____ like a dog - gone ____ king. ____

*Played as even sixteenth notes.

Verse

3. Girl you know I love you so, I can't be - lieve __ I lose con - trol, __

Outro-Guitar Solo

*Chord symbols reflect overall harmony.

**Played behind the beat.

Lost in You

Written by Jimmie Vaughan and Malcom Rebennack

Capo III

Intro

Moderately ♩ = 98

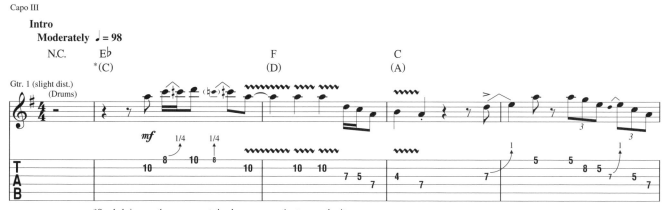

*Symbols in parentheses represent chord names respective to capoed guitar.
Symbols above reflect actual sounding chords. Capoed fret is "0" in tab.
Chord symbols reflect overall harmony.

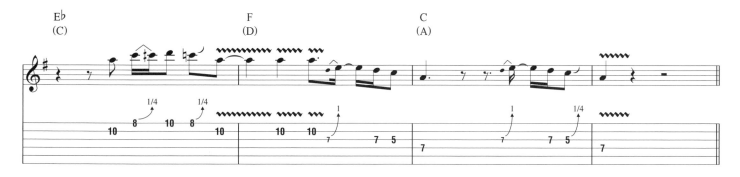

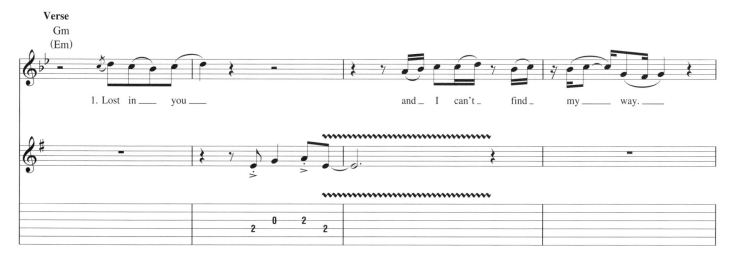

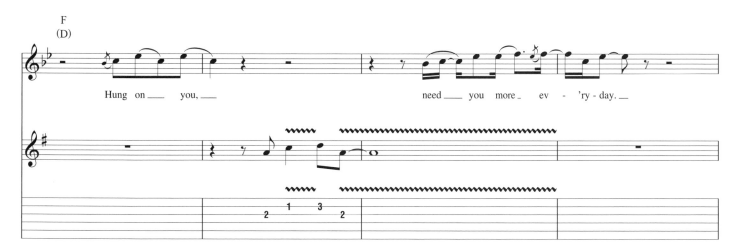

*Played ahead of the beat.

*Played ahead of the beat.

I lose sight. _____ Whoo.

*let ring ---------------- *let ring ---------------------------- let ring ---------------- let ring -|

*Applies to 3rd & 4th strings only.

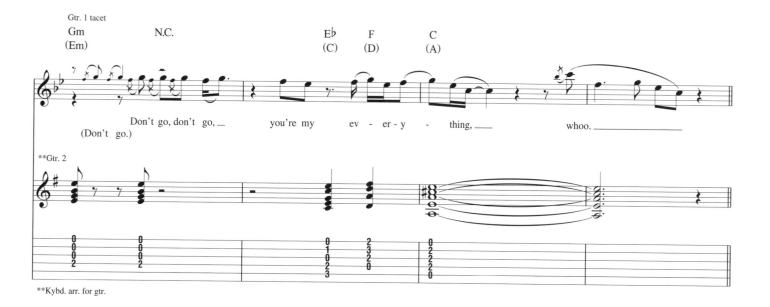

Gtr. 1 tacet
Gm   N.C.   E♭   F   C
(Em)   (C)   (D) (A)

Don't go, don't go, ____ you're my ev - er - y - thing, ____ whoo. _____
(Don't go.)

**Gtr. 2

**Kybd. arr. for gtr.

Guitar Solo

Gtr. 2 tacet
Gm
(Em)
Gtr. 1

mf

F
(D)

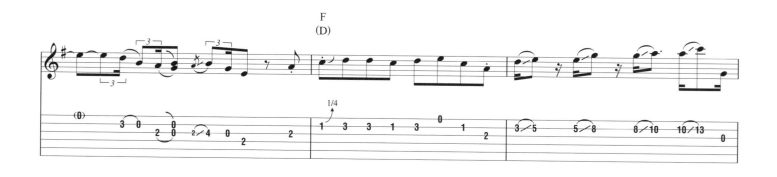

1/4

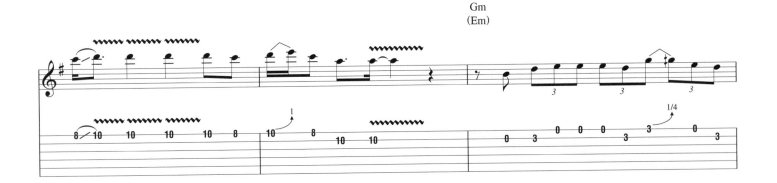

Gm
(Em)

E♭   F   C
(C)   (D) (A)

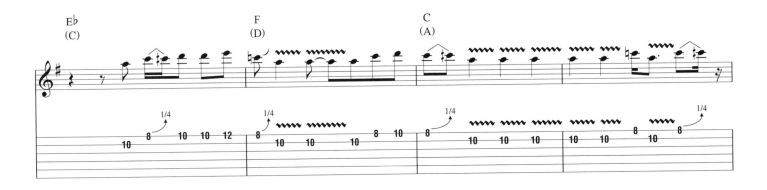

E♭   F   C
(C)   (D) (A)

Outro

E♭   F   C
(C)   (D) (A)

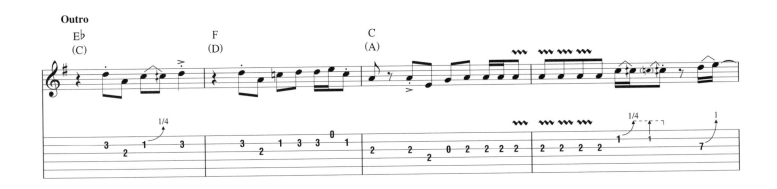

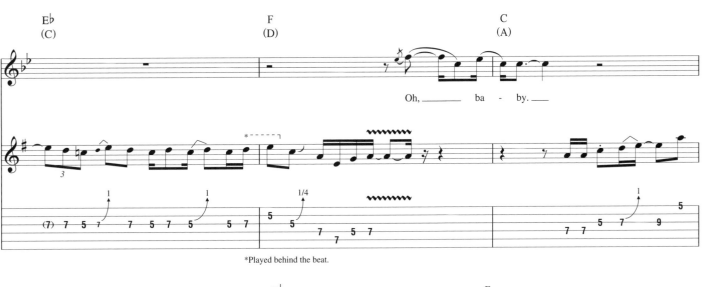

Oh, _____ ba - by. _____

*Played behind the beat.

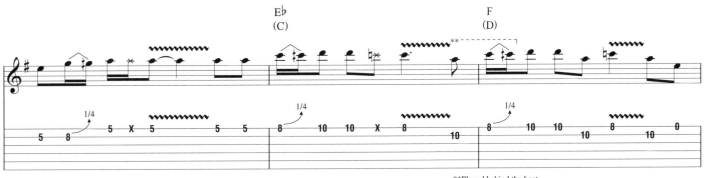

**Played behind the beat.

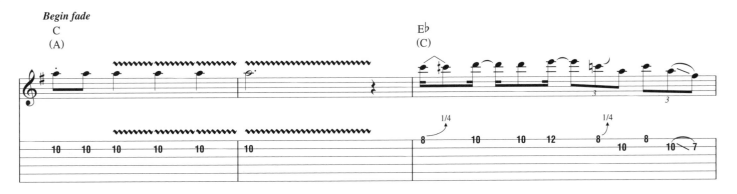

Begin fade

w/ Lead Voc. ad lib. (till fade)

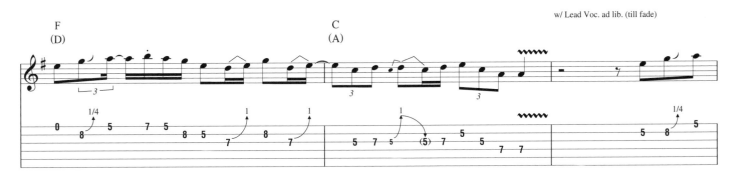

Fade out

She's Tuff

Words and Music by Jerry McCain

%̸ Verse

Moderate Blues ♩ = 109

1. You ought-a see my ba-by when she walk down the street, _ up-set-tin' ev-'ry-
   Pres-i-dent said to my ba-by, come here, sweet-heart, you can stop a war _

Gtr. 1 (clean)

*Chord symbols reflect implied harmony.

2nd time, Gtr. 1: w/ Rhy. Fill 3

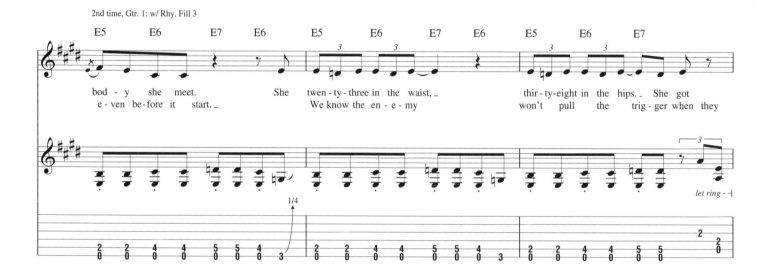

bod-y she meet. She twen-ty-three in the waist, _ thir-ty-eight in the hips. She got
e-ven be-fore it start. _ We know the en-e-my won't pull the trig-ger when they

Rhy. Fill 3
Gtr. 1

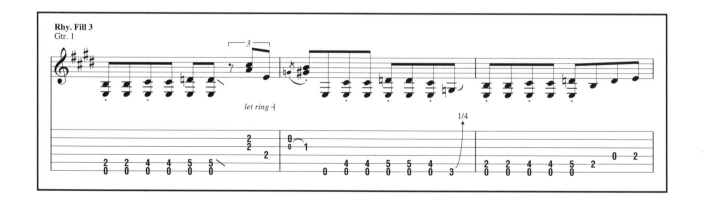

Harmonica Solo

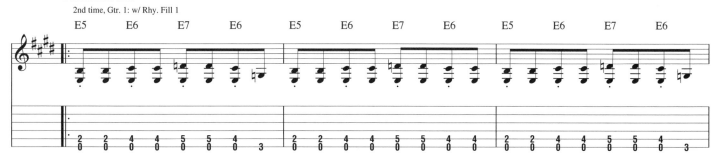

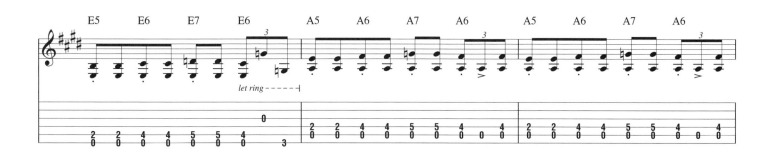

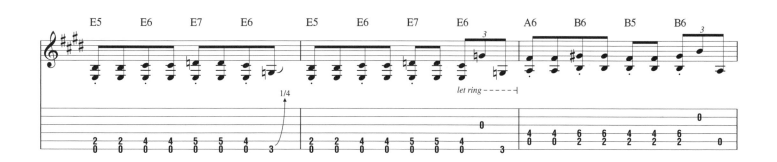

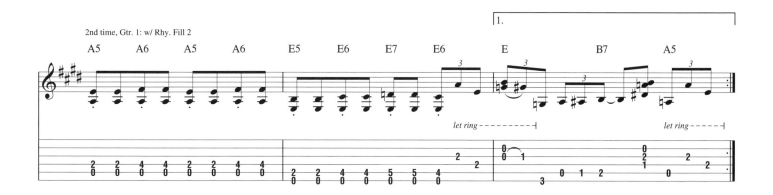

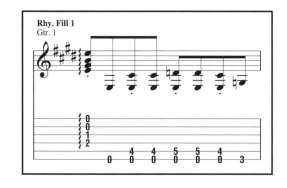

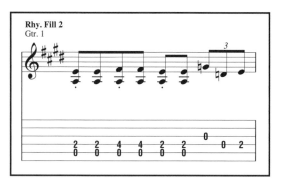

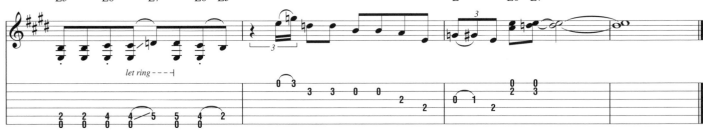

from Jimmie Vaughan - *Strange Pleasure*

Six Strings Down

Written by Jimmie Vaughan, Arthur Neville, Cyril Neville, Eric Kolb and Kelsey Smith

Gtr. 1; Capo III

Intro

Moderate Blues ♩ = 116

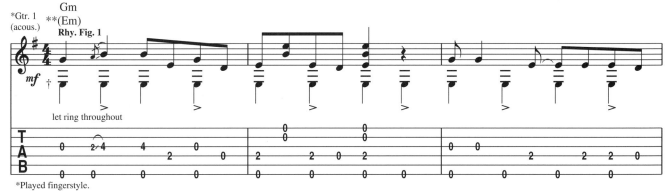

*Played fingerstyle.

**Symbols in parentheses represent chord names respective to capoed gtr. Symbols above reflect actual sounding chords. Capoed fret is "0" in tab.

†P.M. on downstemmed notes only, throughout.

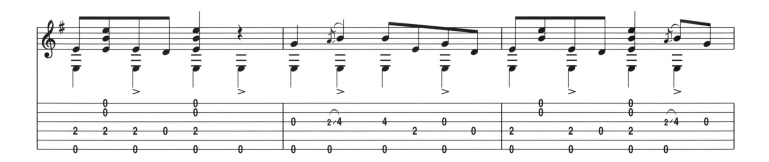

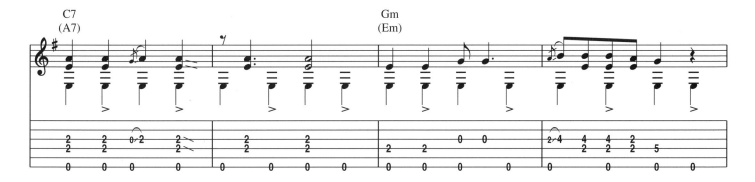

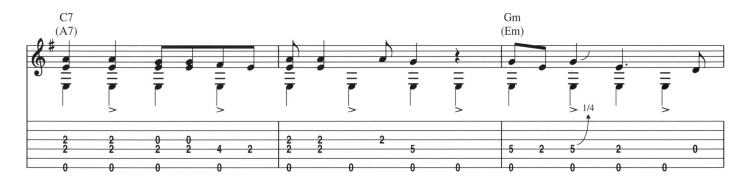

C7   D7   Gm
(A7)   (B7)   (Em)

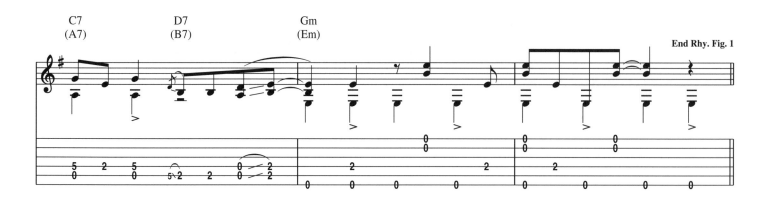

Verse
Gtr. 1: w/ Rhy. Fig. 1
Gm
(Em)

1. Al - pine Val - ley _____ in the mid - dle of the night.

C7
(A7)

Six strings down _____ on the heav - en bound flight. _

*Gtr. 1: w/ Rhy. Fill 1
Gm
(Em)

He's got a pick, a strap, gui - tar on his back.

*Gtr. 1 plays Rhy. Fill 1, then continues in Rhy. Fig. 1.

C7   Gm
(A7)   (Bm)

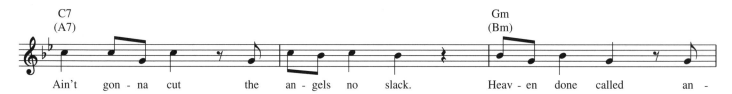

Ain't gon - na cut the an - gels no slack. Heav - en done called an -

**Gtr. 1: w/ Fill 1
C7   D7   Gm
(A7)   (B7)   (Em)

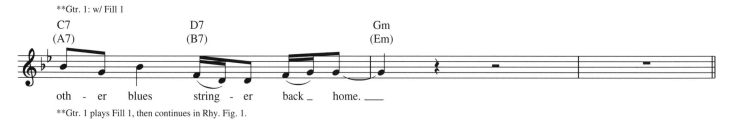

oth - er blues string - er back _ home. ___

**Gtr. 1 plays Fill 1, then continues in Rhy. Fig. 1.

Rhy. Fill 1
Gtr. 1

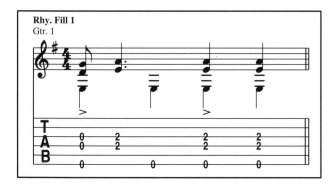

Fill 1
Gtr. 1

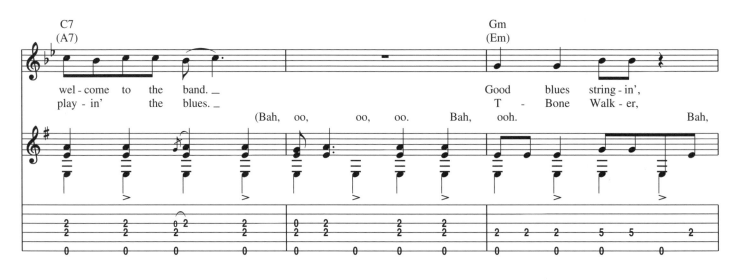

wel - come to the band. __ Good blues string - in',
play - in' the blues. __ T - Bone Walk - er,

(Bah, oo, oo, oo. Bah, ooh. Bah,

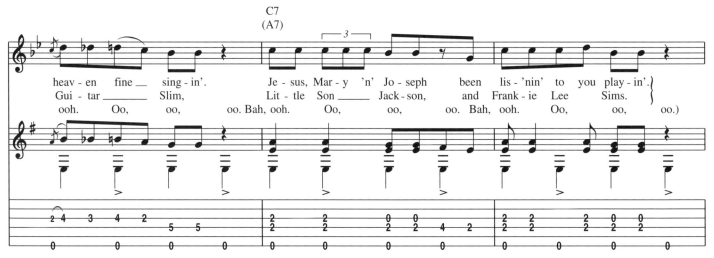

heav - en fine __ sing - in'. Je - sus, Mar - y 'n' Jo - seph been lis - 'nin' to you play - in'.
Gui - tar _____ Slim, Lit - tle Son _____ Jack - son, and Frank - ie Lee Sims.
ooh. Oo, oo, oo. Bah, ooh. Oo, oo, oo. Bah, ooh. Oo, oo, oo.)

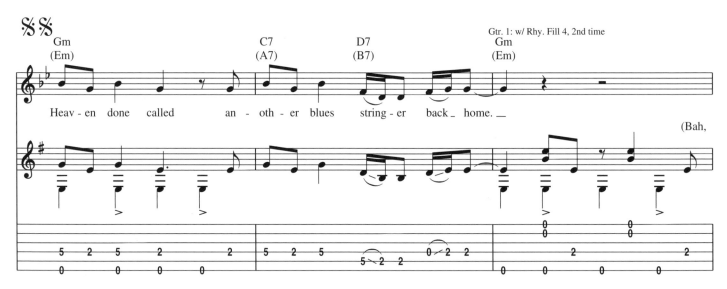

Gtr. 1: w/ Rhy. Fill 4, 2nd time

Heav - en done called an - oth - er blues string - er back __ home. __

(Bah,

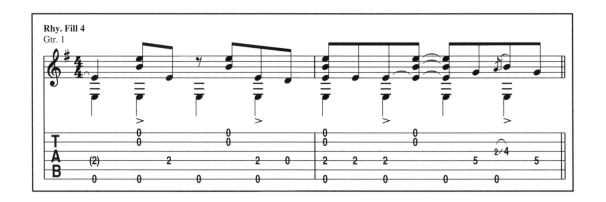

Rhy. Fill 4
Gtr. 1

69

*No P.M. on downstemmed notes, till end.

from The Vaughan Brothers-*Family Style*

Telephone Song

Written by Stevie Ray Vaughan and Doyle Bramhall

Introduction

Moderate Rock ♩ = 118

Tune down 1/2 step:
(low to high) Eb–Ab–Db–Gb–Bb–Eb

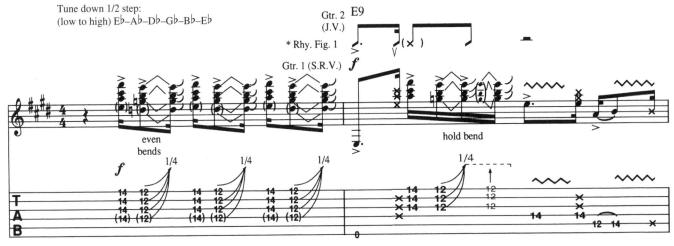

*Rhy. Fig. 1 includes both gtrs.

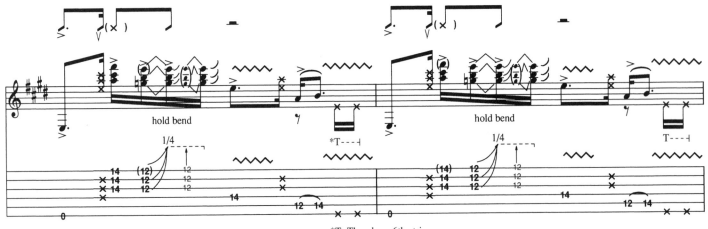

*T=Thumb on 6th string

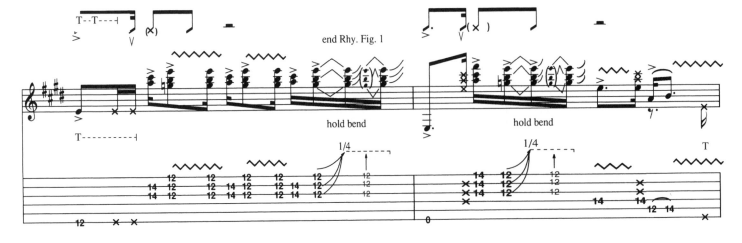

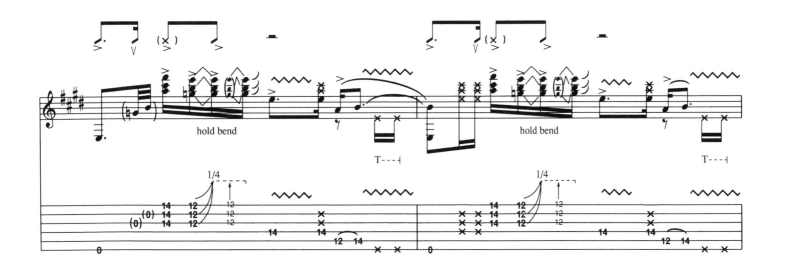

1st Verse

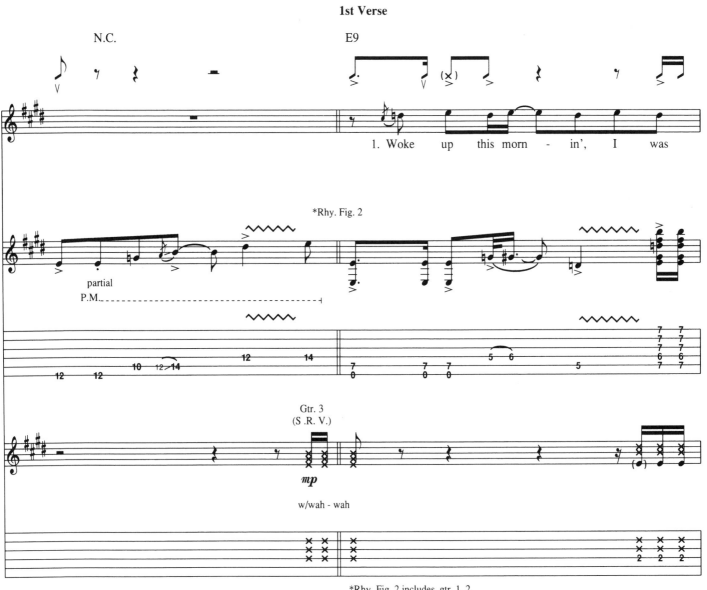

1. Woke up this morn - in', I was

*Rhy. Fig. 2

partial
P.M.

Gtr. 3
(S.R.V.)

mp

w/wah - wah

*Rhy. Fig. 2 includes gtr. 1, 2.

all a - lone. ___ Saw ___ your pic - ture by the tel - e - phone.

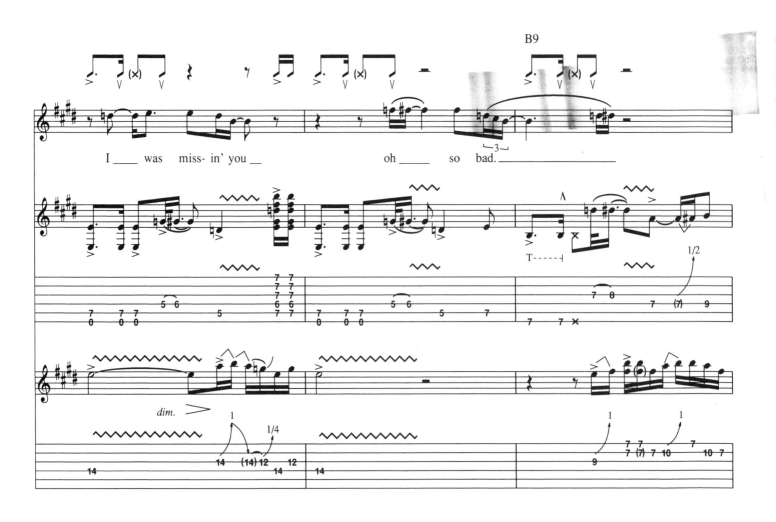

I ___ was miss- in' you ___ oh ___ so bad. ___

Wish ___ I had you

here to hold. _ All I've got is this touch - tone phone.

So __ I __ guess __ I'll __ give __ you __ a __ call. _____

2nd, 3rd Verses

2. Op - er - a - tor,

3. Woke __ up this morn-ing, I was

help _ me please, __   get thru to my ba- by   way o - ver- seas. _____
all a - lone. ___   Saw your pic - ture   by the tel - e - phone. _____

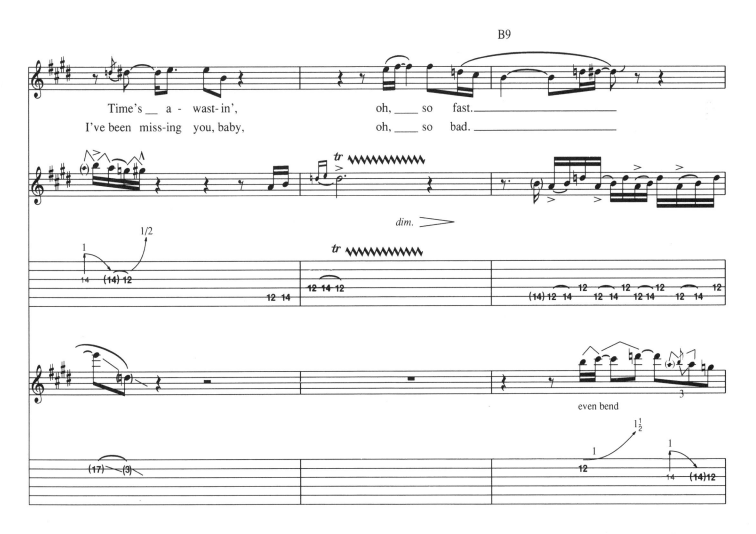

Time's __ a - wast- in',   oh, ___ so fast. _____
I've been miss-ing you, baby,   oh, ____ so bad. _____

E9

Hel - lo ba - by, tell me is that you? ___
I love you ba - by with all my might. ___

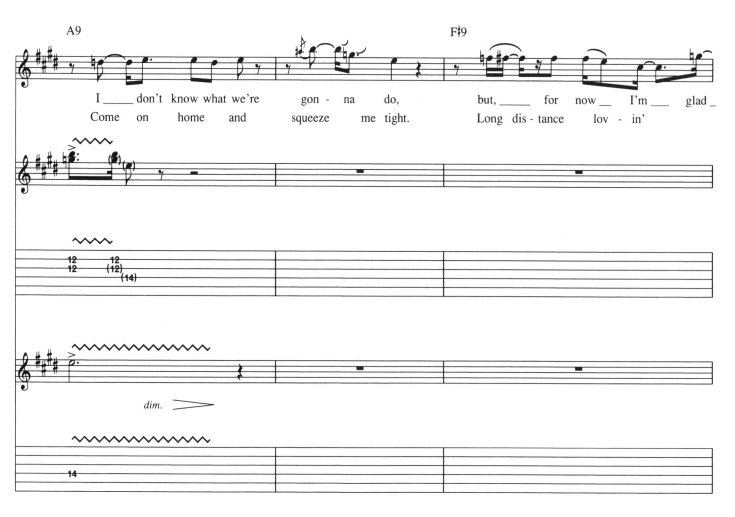

A9   F#9

I ___ don't know what we're gon - na do, but, ___ for now ___ I'm ___ glad ___
Come on home and squeeze me tight. Long dis - tance lov - in'

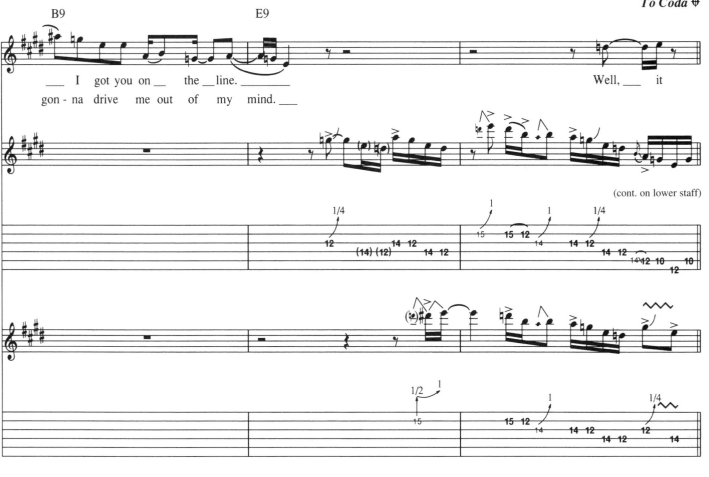

Bridge

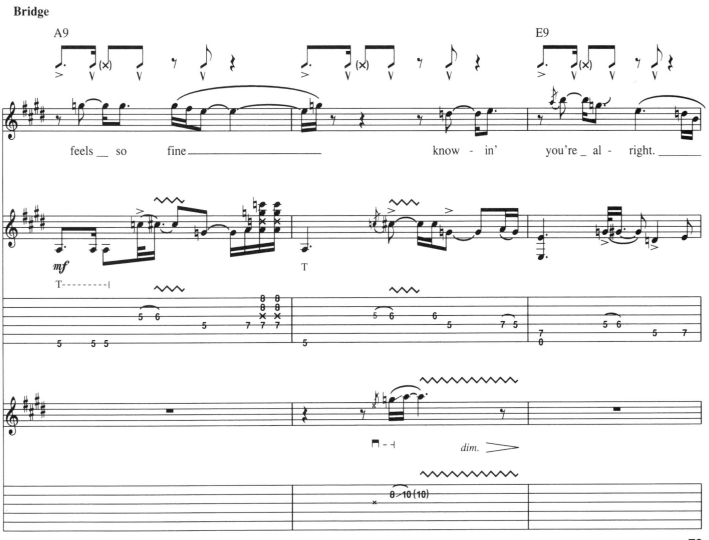

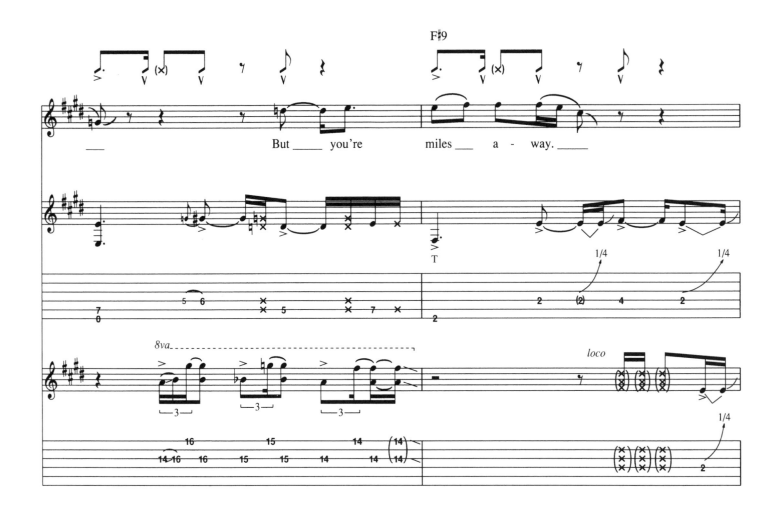

But ____ you're miles ____ a - way. ____

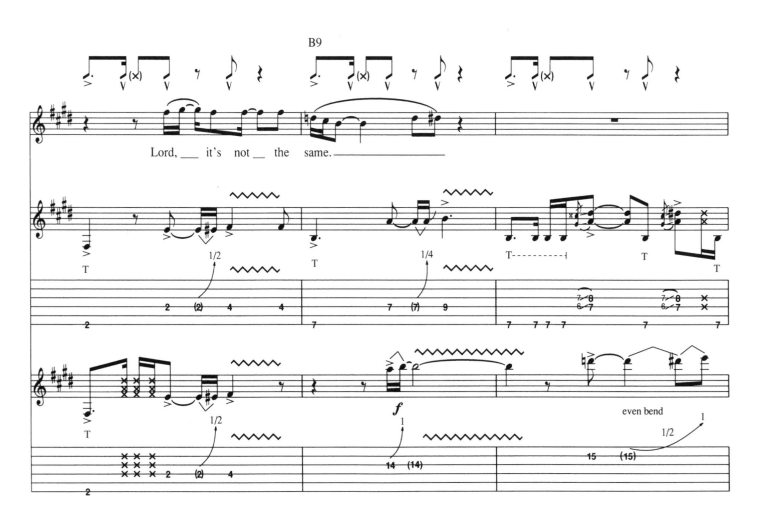

Lord, ___ it's not ___ the same. ____

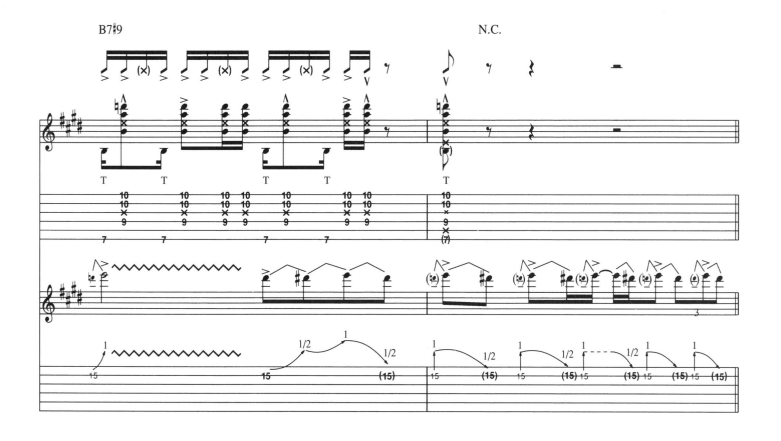

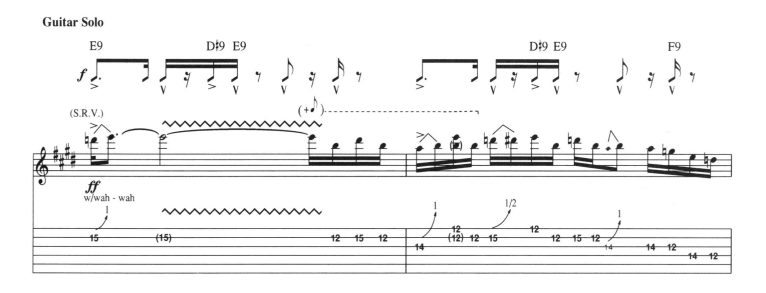

Guitar Solo

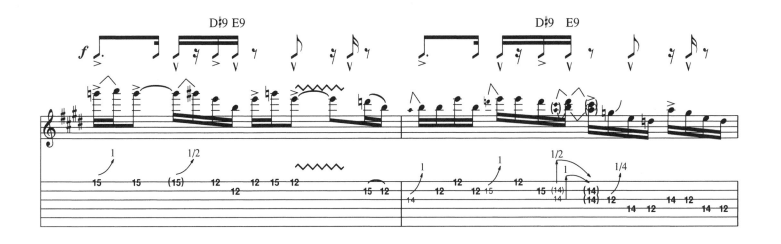

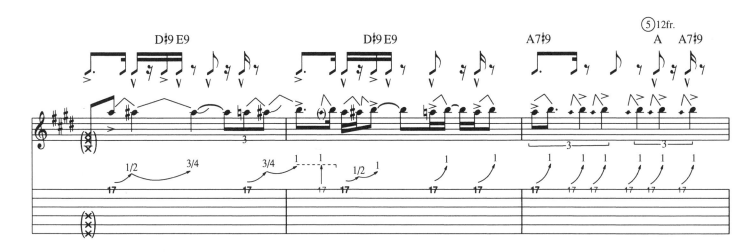

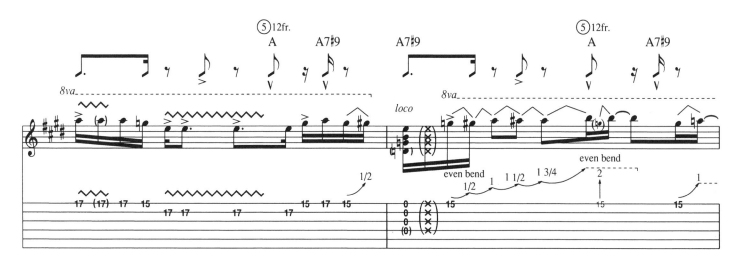

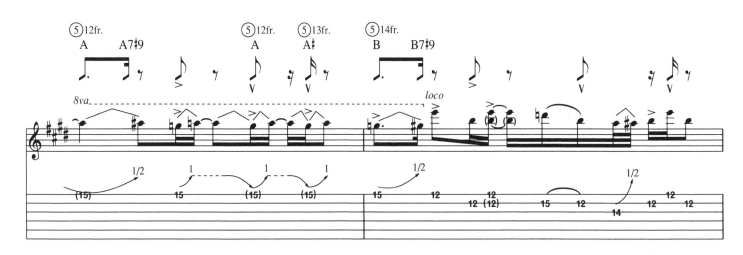

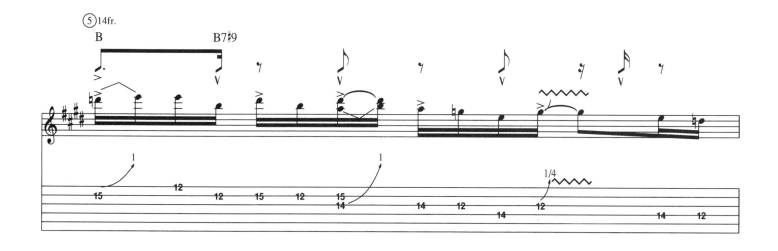

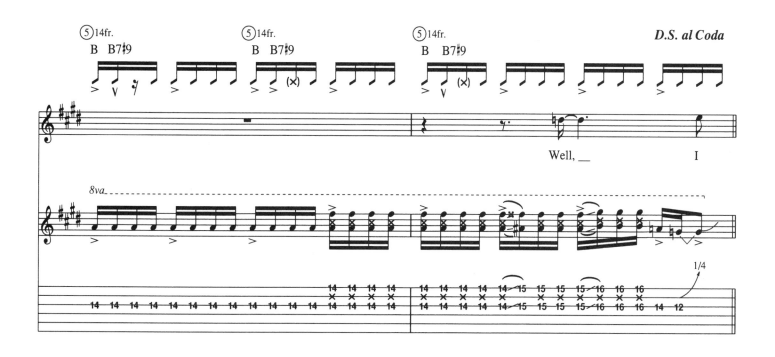

D.S. al Coda

Well, ___ I

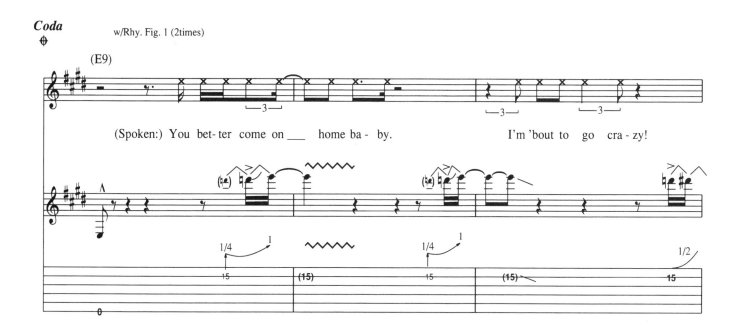

Coda

w/Rhy. Fig. 1 (2times)

(E9)

(Spoken:) You bet-ter come on ___ home ba - by.   I'm 'bout to go cra - zy!

I'm tired ———— of hug - gin' my pil - low

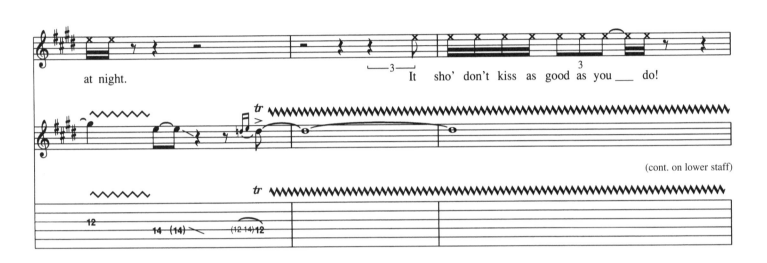

at night.   It sho' don't kiss as good as you ___ do!

(cont. on lower staff)

w/Rhy. Fig. 1 (Gtr. 2 only)

'N' all them pic - tures you gave me.

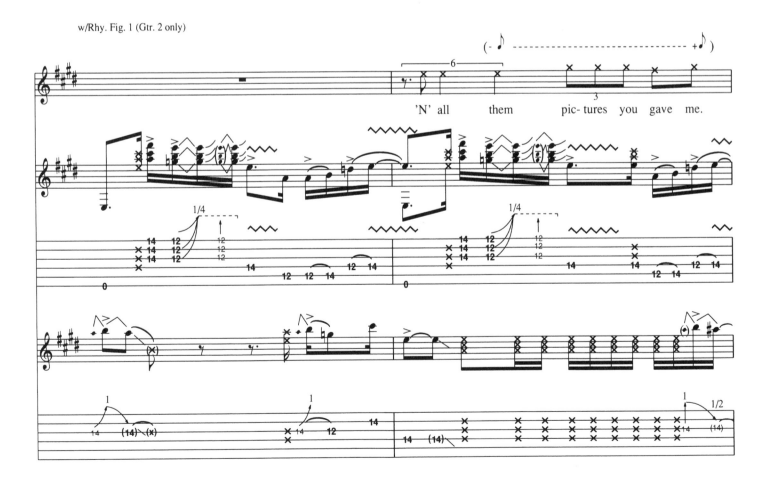

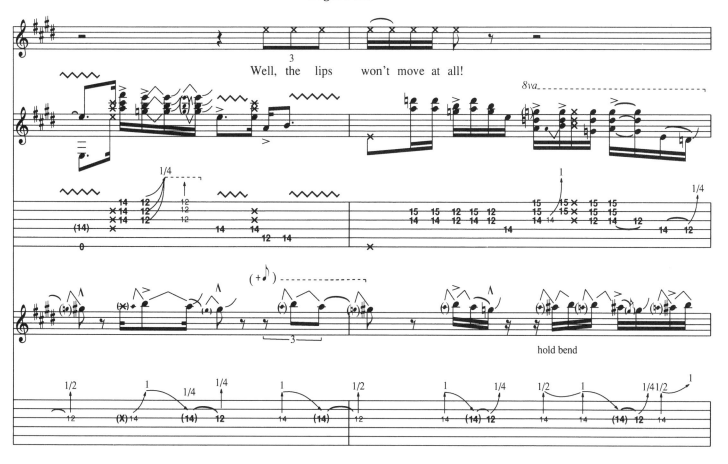

Well, the lips won't move at all!

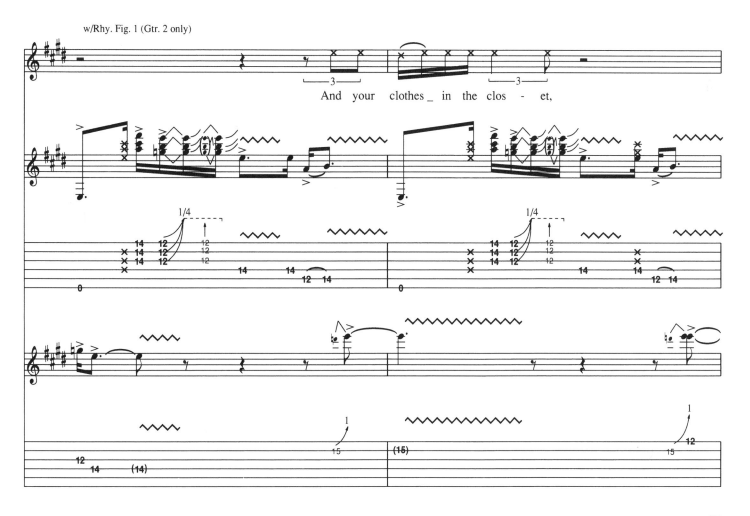

w/Rhy. Fig. 1 (Gtr. 2 only)

And your clothes _ in the clos - et,

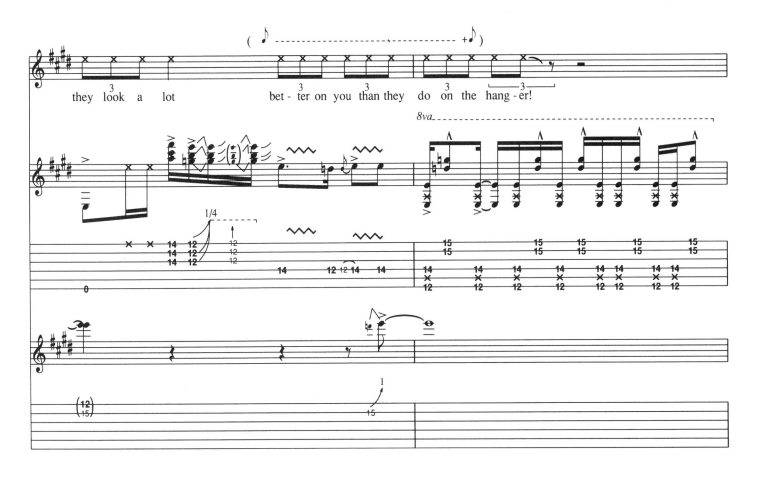

they look a lot bet - ter on you than they do on the hang - er!

w/Rhy. Fig. 1 (Gtr. 1, 2)

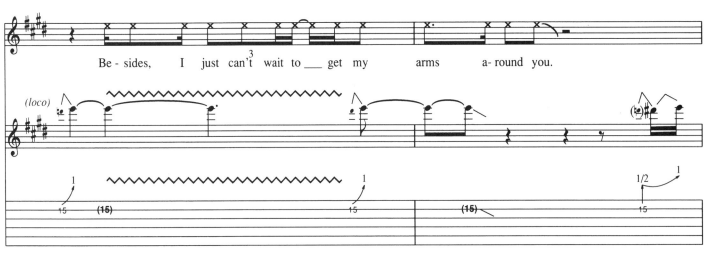

Be - sides, I just can't wait to ___ get my arms a- round you.

Fade out

Come on home!

even bend
dim.

86

Tuff Enuff

Words and Music by Kim Wilson

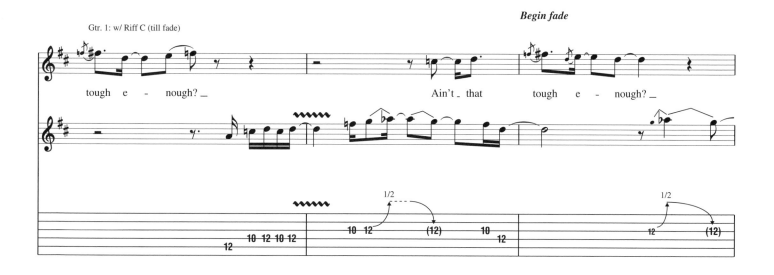

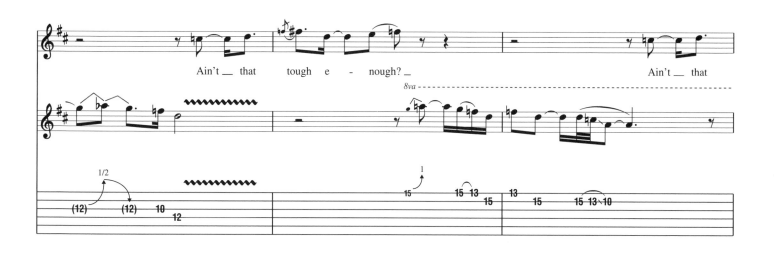

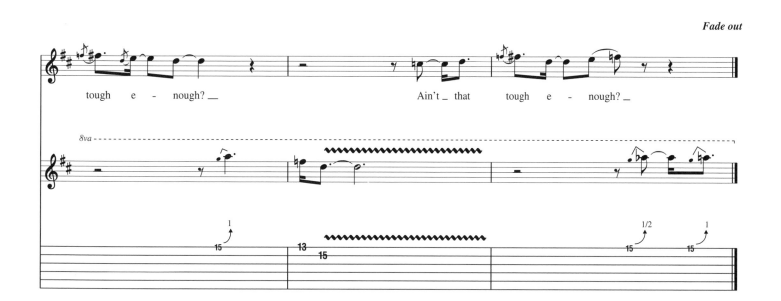

from The Fabulous Thunderbirds - *Girls Go Wild*

Walkin' to My Baby
(Walkin' With My Baby)

Words and Music by Kim Wilson

*Chord symbols reflect implied harmony.

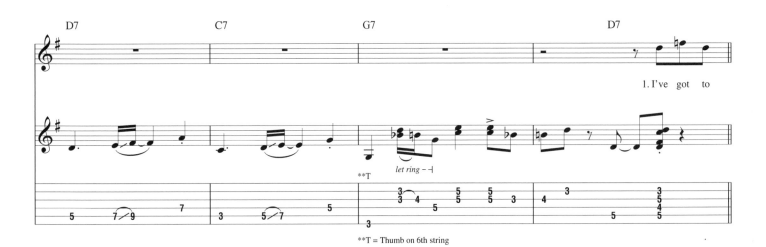

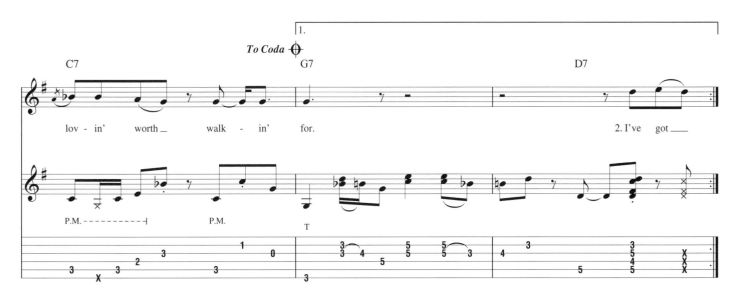

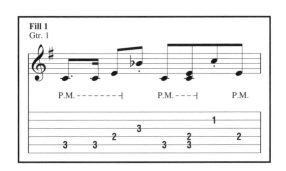

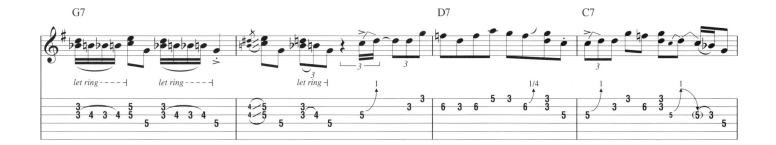

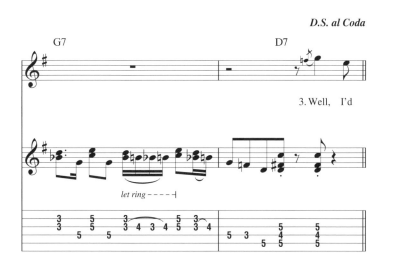

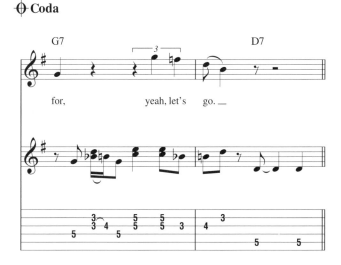

3. Well, I'd

for, yeah, let's go. ____

Outro-Harmonica Solo

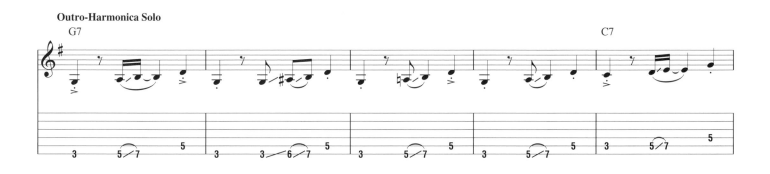

Wrap It Up

Words and Music by Isaac Hayes and David Porter

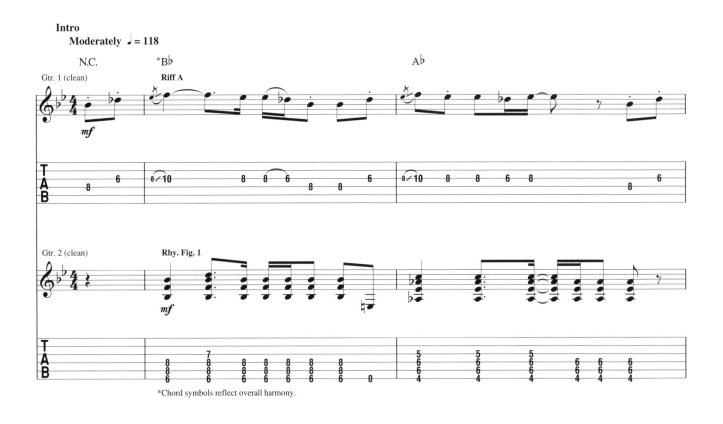

*Chord symbols reflect overall harmony.

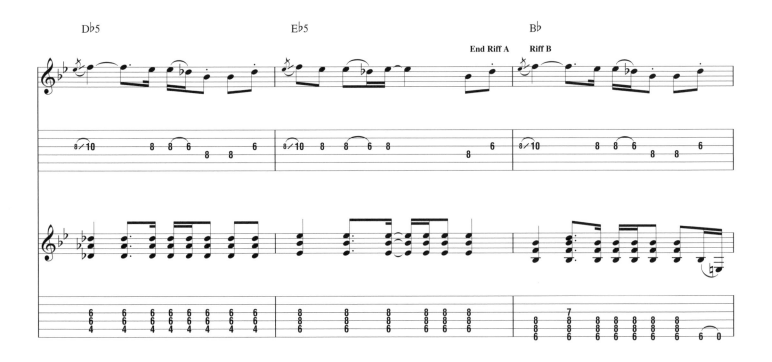

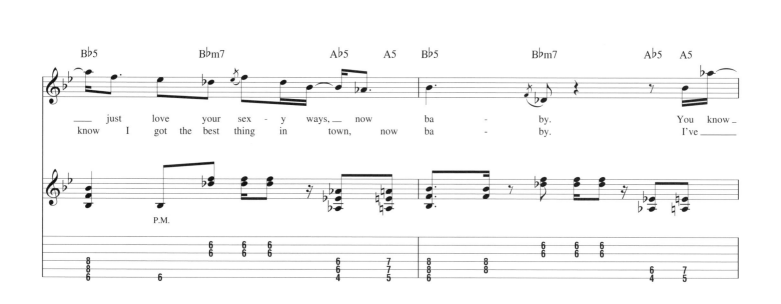

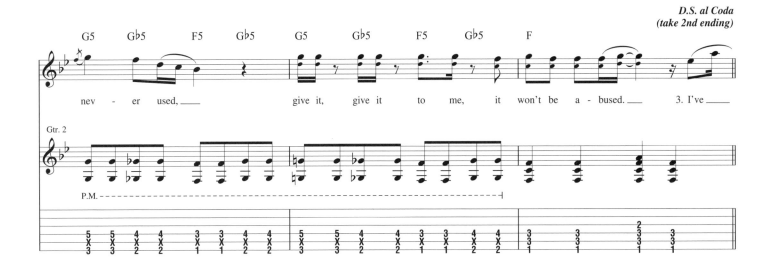

never used, _____ give it, give it to me, it won't be a - bused. ____ 3. I've ____

⊕ Coda

___ it. Wrap, wrap, wrap, wrap, wrap, wrap it up, ___

Outro-Chorus

Gtr. 1: w/ Riff A (2 times)
Gtr. 2: w/ Rhy. Fig. 1

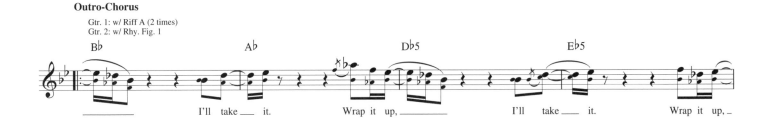

I'll take ____ it. Wrap it up, ____ I'll take ____ it. Wrap it up, ____

Repeat and fade

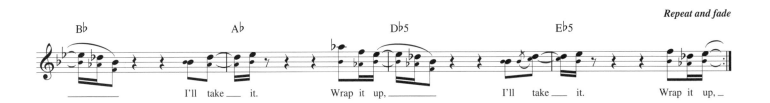

I'll take ____ it. Wrap it up, ____ I'll take ____ it. Wrap it up, ____

Guitar Notation Legend

Guitar Music can be notated three different ways: on a *musical staff*, in *tablature*, and in *rhythm slashes*.

RHYTHM SLASHES are written above the staff. Strum chords in the rhythm indicated. Use the chord diagrams found at the top of the first page of the transcription for the appropriate chord voicings. Round noteheads indicate single notes.

THE MUSICAL STAFF shows pitches and rhythms and is divided by bar lines into measures. Pitches are named after the first seven letters of the alphabet.

TABLATURE graphically represents the guitar fingerboard. Each horizontal line represents a a string, and each number represents a fret.

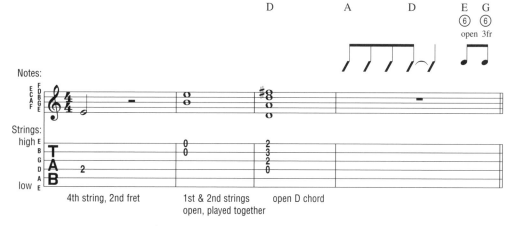

4th string, 2nd fret

1st & 2nd strings open, played together

open D chord

Definitions for Special Guitar Notation

HALF-STEP BEND: Strike the note and bend up 1/2 step.

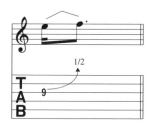

WHOLE-STEP BEND: Strike the note and bend up one step.

GRACE NOTE BEND: Strike the note and immediately bend up as indicated.

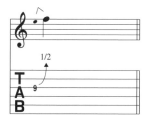

SLIGHT (MICROTONE) BEND: Strike the note and bend up 1/4 step.

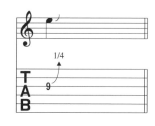

BEND AND RELEASE: Strike the note and bend up as indicated, then release back to the original note. Only the first note is struck.

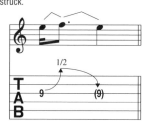

PRE-BEND: Bend the note as indicated, then strike it.

PRE-BEND AND RELEASE: Bend the note as indicated. Strike it and release the bend back to the original note.

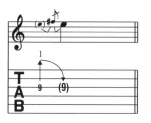

UNISON BEND: Strike the two notes simultaneously and bend the lower note up to the pitch of the higher.

VIBRATO: The string is vibrated by rapidly bending and releasing the note with the fretting hand.

WIDE VIBRATO: The pitch is varied to a greater degree by vibrating with the fretting hand.

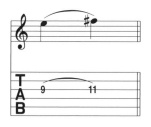

HAMMER-ON: Strike the first (lower) note with one finger, then sound the higher note (on the same string) with another finger by fretting it without picking.

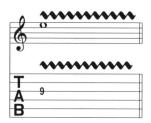

PULL-OFF: Place both fingers on the notes to be sounded. Strike the first note and without picking, pull the finger off to sound the second (lower) note.

LEGATO SLIDE: Strike the first note and then slide the same fret-hand finger up or down to the second note. The second note is not struck.

SHIFT SLIDE: Same as legato slide, except the second note is struck.

TRILL: Very rapidly alternate between the notes indicated by continuously hammering on and pulling off.

TAPPING: Hammer ("tap") the fret indicated with the pick-hand index or middle finger and pull off to the note fretted by the fret hand.

NATURAL HARMONIC: Strike the note while the fret-hand lightly touches the string directly over the fret indicated.

PINCH HARMONIC: The note is fretted normally and a harmonic is produced by adding the edge of the thumb or the tip of the index finger of the pick hand to the normal pick attack.

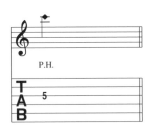

HARP HARMONIC: The note is fretted normally and a harmonic is produced by gently resting the pick hand's index finger directly above the indicated fret (in parentheses) while the pick hand's thumb or pick assists by plucking the appropriate string.

PICK SCRAPE: The edge of the pick is rubbed down (or up) the string, producing a scratchy sound.

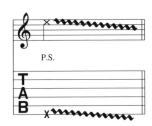

MUFFLED STRINGS: A percussive sound is produced by laying the fret hand across the string(s) without depressing, and striking them with the pick hand.

PALM MUTING: The note is partially muted by the pick hand lightly touching the string(s) just before the bridge.

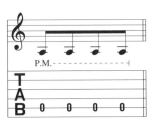

RAKE: Drag the pick across the strings indicated with a single motion.

TREMOLO PICKING: The note is picked as rapidly and continuously as possible.

ARPEGGIATE: Play the notes of the chord indicated by quickly rolling them from bottom to top.

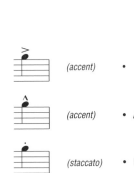

VIBRATO BAR DIVE AND RETURN: The pitch of the note or chord is dropped a specified number of steps (in rhythm) then returned to the original pitch.

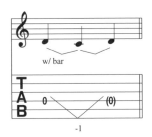

VIBRATO BAR SCOOP: Depress the bar just before striking the note, then quickly release the bar.

VIBRATO BAR DIP: Strike the note and then immediately drop a specified number of steps, then release back to the original pitch.

Additional Musical Definitions

>	*(accent)*	• Accentuate note (play it louder)
∧	*(accent)*	• Accentuate note with great intensity
.	*(staccato)*	• Play the note short
⊓		• Downstroke
∨		• Upstroke
D.S. al Coda		• Go back to the sign (𝄋), then play until the measure marked "***To Coda,***" then skip to the section labelled "**Coda.**"
D.C. al Fine		• Go back to the beginning of the song and play until the measure marked "***Fine***" (end).

Rhy. Fig.	• Label used to recall a recurring accompaniment pattern (usually chordal).
Riff	• Label used to recall composed, melodic lines (usually single notes) which recur.
Fill	• Label used to identify a brief melodic figure which is to be inserted into the arrangement.
Rhy. Fill	• A chordal version of a Fill.
tacet	• Instrument is silent (drops out).
	• Repeat measures between signs.
1. 2.	• When a repeated section has different endings, play the first ending only the first time and the second ending only the second time.

NOTE: Tablature numbers in parentheses mean:
1. The note is being sustained over a system (note in standard notation is tied), or
2. The note is sustained, but a new articulation (such as a hammer-on, pull-off, slide or vibrato begins), or
3. The note is a barely audible "ghost" note (note in standard notation is also in parentheses).

RECORDED VERSIONS®

The Best Note-For-Note Transcriptions Available

ALL BOOKS INCLUDE TABLATURE

00692015 Aerosmith – Greatest Hits $22.95
00690603 Aerosmith – O Yeah! (Ultimate Hits) $24.95
00690178 Alice in Chains – Acoustic $19.95
00694865 Alice in Chains – Dirt $19.95
00690387 Alice in Chains – Nothing Safe: The Best of the Box $19.95
00690812 All American Rejects – Move Along $19.95
00694932 Allman Brothers Band – Volume 1 ......$24.95
00694933 Allman Brothers Band – Volume 2 ......$24.95
00694934 Allman Brothers Band – Volume 3 ......$24.95
00690755 Alter Bridge – One Day Remains $19.95
00690609 Audioslave $19.95
00690804 Audioslave – Out of Exile $19.95
00690366 Bad Company – Original Anthology, Book 1 ...$19.95
00690503 Beach Boys – Very Best of $19.95
00690489 Beatles – 1 ....$24.95
00694929 Beatles – 1962-1966 ....$24.95
00694930 Beatles – 1967-1970 ....$24.95
00694832 Beatles – For Acoustic Guitar $22.95
00690110 Beatles – White Album (Book 1) $19.95
00690792 Beck – Guero $19.95
00692385 Berry, Chuck $19.95
00692200 Black Sabbath – We Sold Our Soul for Rock 'N' Roll $19.95
00690674 Blink-182 ....$19.95
00690389 Blink-182 – Enema of the State $19.95
00690523 Blink-182 – Take Off Your Pants & Jacket ..$19.95
00690491 Bowie, David – Best of $19.95
00690764 Breaking Benjamin – We Are Not Alone ..$19.95
00690451 Buckley, Jeff – Collection $24.95
00690590 Clapton, Eric – Anthology $29.95
00690415 Clapton Chronicles – Best of Eric Clapton ..$18.95
00690074 Clapton, Eric – The Cream of Clapton $24.95
00690716 Clapton, Eric – Me and Mr. Johnson $19.95
00694869 Clapton, Eric – Unplugged $22.95
00690162 Clash – Best of The $19.95
00690593 Coldplay – A Rush of Blood to the Head ..$19.95
00690806 Coldplay – X & Y $19.95
00694940 Counting Crows – August & Everything After ..$19.95
00690401 Creed – Human Clay $19.95
00690352 Creed – My Own Prison $19.95
00690551 Creed – Weathered $19.95
00690648 Croce, Jim – Very Best of $19.95
00690572 Cropper, Steve – Soul Man $19.95
00690613 Crosby, Stills & Nash – Best of $19.95
00690777 Crossfade $19.95
00690289 Deep Purple – Best of $17.95
00690347 Doors, The – Anthology $22.95
00690348 Doors, The – Essential Guitar Collection ..$16.95
00690810 Fall Out Boy – From Under the Cork Tree ..$19.95
00690664 Fleetwood Mac – Best of $19.95
00690808 Foo Fighters – In Your Honor $19.95
00694920 Free – Best of $19.95
00690773 Good Charlotte – The Chronicles of Life and Death $19.95
00690601 Good Charlotte – The Young and the Hopeless $19.95
00690697 Hall, Jim – Best of $19.95
00694798 Harrison, George – Anthology $19.95
00690778 Hawk Nelson – Letters to the President ...$19.95
00692930 Hendrix, Jimi – Are You Experienced? $24.95
00692931 Hendrix, Jimi – Axis: Bold As Love $22.95
00690608 Hendrix, Jimi – Blue Wild Angel $24.95
00692932 Hendrix, Jimi – Electric Ladyland $24.95
00690017 Hendrix, Jimi – Live at Woodstock $24.95
00690602 Hendrix, Jimi – Smash Hits $19.95
00690692 Idol, Billy – Very Best of $19.95
00690688 Incubus – A Crow Left of the Murder $19.95
00690457 Incubus – Make Yourself $19.95
00690544 Incubus – Morningview $19.95
00690730 Jackson, Alan – Guitar Collection $19.95
00690721 Jet – Get Born $19.95
00690684 Jethro Tull – Aqualung $19.95
00690647 Jewel – Best of $19.95
00690751 John5 – Vertigo $19.95
00690271 Johnson, Robert – New Transcriptions ...$24.95
00699131 Joplin, Janis – Best of $19.95
00690427 Judas Priest – Best of $19.95
00690742 Killers, The – Hot Fuss $19.95
00694903 Kiss – Best of $24.95
00690780 Korn – Greatest Hits, Volume 1 ....$22.95
00690726 Lavigne, Avril – Under My Skin $19.95
00690679 Lennon, John – Guitar Collection $19.95
00690785 Limp Bizkit – Best of $19.95
00690781 Linkin Park – Hybrid Theory $22.95
00690782 Linkin Park – Meteora $22.95
00690783 Live, Best of $19.95
00690743 Los Lonely Boys $19.95
00690720 Lostprophets – Start Something $19.95
00694954 Lynyrd Skynyrd – New Best of $19.95
00690577 Malmsteen, Yngwie – Anthology $24.95
00690754 Manson, Marilyn – Lest We Forget $19.95
00694956 Marley, Bob – Legend $19.95
00694945 Marley, Bob – Songs of Freedom $24.95
00690748 Maroon5 – 1.22.03 Acoustic $19.95
00690657 Maroon5 – Songs About Jane $19.95
00120080 McLean, Don – Songbook $19.95
00694951 Megadeth – Rust in Peace $22.95
00690768 Megadeth – The System Has Failed $19.95
00690505 Mellencamp, John – Guitar Collection $19.95
00690646 Metheny, Pat – One Quiet Night $19.95
00690565 Metheny, Pat – Rejoicing $19.95
00690558 Metheny, Pat – Trio: 99>00 ....$19.95
00690561 Metheny, Pat – Trio > Live $22.95
00690040 Miller, Steve, Band – Young Hearts $19.95
00690769 Modest Mouse – Good News for People Who Love Bad News $19.95
00690786 Mudvayne – The End of All Things to Come ..$22.95
00690787 Mudvayne – L.D. 50 ....$22.95
00690794 Mudvayne – Lost and Found $19.95
00690611 Nirvana $22.95
00694883 Nirvana – Nevermind $19.95
00690026 Nirvana – Unplugged in New York $19.95
00690739 No Doubt – Rock Steady $22.95
00690807 Offspring, The – Greatest Hits $19.95
00694847 Osbourne, Ozzy – Best of $22.95
00690399 Osbourne, Ozzy – Ozzman Cometh $19.95
00694855 Pearl Jam – Ten $19.95
00690439 Perfect Circle, A – Mer De Noms $19.95
00690661 Perfect Circle, A – Thirteenth Step $19.95
00690499 Petty, Tom – Definitive Guitar Collection ..$19.95
00690731 Pillar – Where Do We Go from Here? $19.95
00690428 Pink Floyd – Dark Side of the Moon $19.95
00693864 Police, The – Best of $19.95
00694975 Queen – Greatest Hits $24.95
00690670 Queensryche – Very Best of $19.95
00694910 Rage Against the Machine $19.95
00690055 Red Hot Chili Peppers – Bloodsugarsexmagik $19.95
00690584 Red Hot Chili Peppers – By the Way $19.95
00690379 Red Hot Chili Peppers – Californication ..$19.95
00690673 Red Hot Chili Peppers – Greatest Hits $19.95
00690511 Reinhardt, Django – Definitive Collection ..$19.95
00690779 Relient K – MMHMM $19.95
00690643 Relient K – Two Lefts Don't Make a Right...But Three Do $19.95
00690631 Rolling Stones – Guitar Anthology $24.95
00690685 Roth, David Lee – Eat 'Em and Smile $19.95
00690694 Roth, David Lee – Guitar Anthology $24.95
00690749 Saliva – Survival of the Sickest $19.95
00690031 Santana's Greatest Hits $19.95
00690796 Schenker, Michael – Very Best of $19.95
00690566 Scorpions – Best of $19.95
00690604 Seger, Bob – Guitar Collection $19.95
00690530 Slipknot – Iowa $19.95
00690733 Slipknot – Vol. 3 (The Subliminal Verses) ..$19.95
00690691 Smashing Pumpkins Anthology $19.95
00120004 Steely Dan – Best of $24.95
00694921 Steppenwolf – Best of $22.95
00690655 Stern, Mike – Best of $19.95
00690689 Story of the Year – Page Avenue $19.95
00690520 Styx Guitar Collection $19.95
00120081 Sublime $19.95
00690519 SUM 41 – All Killer No Filler $19.95
00690771 SUM 41 – Chuck $19.95
00690767 Switchfoot – The Beautiful Letdown $19.95
00690815 Switchfoot – Nothing Is Sound $19.95
00690799 System of a Down – Mezmerize $19.95
00690531 System of a Down – Toxicity $19.95
00694824 Taylor, James – Best of $16.95
00690737 3 Doors Down – The Better Life $22.95
00690776 3 Doors Down – Seventeen Days $19.95
00690683 Trower, Robin – Bridge of Sighs $19.95
00690740 Twain, Shania – Guitar Collection $19.95
00699191 U2 – Best of: 1980-1990 ....$19.95
00690732 U2 – Best of: 1990-2000 ....$19.95
00690775 U2 – How to Dismantle an Atomic Bomb ..$22.95
00694411 U2 – The Joshua Tree $19.95
00660137 Vai, Steve – Passion & Warfare $24.95
00690370 Vaughan, Stevie Ray and Double Trouble – The Real Deal: Greatest Hits Volume 2 ..$22.95
00690116 Vaughan, Stevie Ray – Guitar Collection ...$24.95
00660058 Vaughan, Stevie Ray – Lightnin' Blues 1983-1987 ....$24.95
00694835 Vaughan, Stevie Ray – The Sky Is Crying ..$22.95
00690015 Vaughan, Stevie Ray – Texas Flood $19.95
00690772 Velvet Revolver – Contraband $22.95
00690071 Weezer (The Blue Album) $19.95
00690800 Weezer – Make Believe $19.95
00690447 Who, The – Best of $24.95
00690672 Williams, Dar – Best of $19.95
00690710 Yellowcard – Ocean Avenue $19.95
00690589 ZZ Top Guitar Anthology $22.95

Prices and availability subject to change without notice.
Some products may not be available outside the U.S.A.

FOR A COMPLETE LIST OF GUITAR RECORDED VERSIONS TITLES, SEE YOUR LOCAL MUSIC DEALER, OR WRITE TO:

HAL•LEONARD® CORPORATION
7777 W. BLUEMOUND RD. P.O. BOX 13819 MILWAUKEE, WI 53213

Visit Hal Leonard online at **www.halleonard.com** 0106

HAL·LEONARD GUITAR PLAY·ALONG

This series will help you play your favorite songs quickly and easily. Just follow the tab and listen to the CD to hear how the guitar should sound, and then play along using the separate backing tracks. Mac or PC users can also slow down the tempo without changing pitch by using the CD in their computer. The melody and lyrics are included in the book so that you can sing or simply follow along.

INCLUDES TAB

VOL. 1 – ROCK GUITAR 00699570 / $14.95
Day Tripper • Message in a Bottle • Refugee • Shattered • Sunshine of Your Love • Takin' Care of Business • Tush • Walk This Way.

VOL. 2 – ACOUSTIC 00699569 / $14.95
Angie • Behind Blue Eyes • Best of My Love • Blackbird • Dust in the Wind • Layla • Night Moves • Yesterday.

VOL. 3 – HARD ROCK 00699573 / $14.95
Crazy Train • Iron Man • Living After Midnight • Rock You like a Hurricane • Round and Round • Smoke on the Water • Sweet Child O' Mine • You Really Got Me.

VOL. 4 – POP/ROCK 00699571 / $14.95
Breakdown • Crazy Little Thing Called Love • Hit Me with Your Best Shot • I Want You to Want Me • Lights • R.O.C.K. in the U.S.A. • Summer of '69 • What I Like About You.

VOL. 5 – MODERN ROCK 00699574 / $14.95
Aerials • Alive • Bother • Chop Suey! • Control • Last Resort • Take a Look Around (Theme from *M:I-2*) • Wish You Were Here.

VOL. 6 – '90S ROCK 00699572 / $14.95
Are You Gonna Go My Way • Come Out and Play • I'll Stick Around • Know Your Enemy • Man in the Box • Outshined • Smells Like Teen Spirit • Under the Bridge.

VOL. 7 – BLUES GUITAR 00699575 / $14.95
All Your Love (I Miss Loving) • Born Under a Bad Sign • Hide Away • I'm Tore Down • I'm Your Hoochie Coochie Man • Pride and Joy • Sweet Home Chicago • The Thrill Is Gone.

VOL. 8 – ROCK 00699585 / $14.95
All Right Now • Black Magic Woman • Get Back • Hey Joe • Layla • Love Me Two Times • Won't Get Fooled Again • You Really Got Me.

VOL. 9 – PUNK ROCK 00699576 / $14.95
All the Small Things • Fat Lip • Flavor of the Weak • I Feel So • Lifestyles of the Rich and Famous• Say It Ain't So • Self Esteem • (So) Tired of Waiting for You.

VOL. 10 – ACOUSTIC 00699586 / $14.95
Here Comes the Sun • Landslide • The Magic Bus • Norwegian Wood (This Bird Has Flown) • Pink Houses • Space Oddity • Tangled Up in Blue • Tears in Heaven.

VOL. 11 – EARLY ROCK 00699579 / $14.95
Fun, Fun, Fun • Hound Dog • Louie, Louie • No Particular Place to Go • Oh, Pretty Woman • Rock Around the Clock • Under the Boardwalk • Wild Thing.

VOL. 12 – POP/ROCK 00699587 / $14.95
867-5309/Jenny • Every Breath You Take • Money for Nothing • Rebel, Rebel • Run to You • Ticket to Ride • Wonderful Tonight • You Give Love a Bad Name.

VOL. 13 – FOLK ROCK 00699581 / $14.95
Annie's Song • Leaving on a Jet Plane • Suite: Judy Blue Eyes • This Land Is Your Land • Time in a Bottle • Turn! Turn! Turn! • You've Got a Friend • You've Got to Hide Your Love Away.

VOL. 14 – BLUES ROCK 00699582 / $14.95
Blue on Black • Crossfire • Cross Road Blues (Crossroads) • The House Is Rockin' • La Grange • Move It on Over • Roadhouse Blues • Statesboro Blues.

VOL. 15 – R&B 00699583 / $14.95
Ain't Too Proud to Beg • Brick House • Get Ready • I Can't Help Myself • I Got You (I Feel Good) • I Heard It Through the Grapevine • My Girl • Shining Star.

VOL. 16 – JAZZ 00699584 / $14.95
All Blues • Bluesette • Footprints • How Insensitive • Misty • Satin Doll • Stella by Starlight • Tenor Madness.

VOL. 17 – COUNTRY 00699588 / $14.95
Amie • Boot Scootin' Boogie • Chattahoochee • Folsom Prison Blues • Friends in Low Places • Forever and Ever, Amen • T-R-O-U-B-L-E • Workin' Man Blues.

VOL. 18 – ACOUSTIC ROCK 00699577 / $14.95
About a Girl • Breaking the Girl • Drive • Iris • More Than Words • Patience • Silent Lucidity • 3 AM.

VOL. 19 – SOUL 00699578 / $14.95
Get Up (I Feel Like Being) a Sex Machine • Green Onions • In the Midnight Hour • Knock on Wood • Mustang Sally • Respect • (Sittin' On) the Dock of the Bay • Soul Man.

VOL. 20 – ROCKABILLY 00699580 / $14.95
Be-Bop-A-Lula • Blue Suede Shoes • Hello Mary Lou • Little Sister • Mystery Train • Rock This Town • Stray Cat Strut • That'll Be the Day.

VOL. 21 – YULETIDE 00699602 / $14.95
Angels We Have Heard on High • Away in a Manger • Deck the Hall • The First Noel • Go, Tell It on the Mountain • Jingle Bells • Joy to the World • O Little Town of Bethlehem.

VOL. 22 – CHRISTMAS 00699600 / $14.95
The Christmas Song • Frosty the Snow Man • Happy Xmas • Here Comes Santa Claus • Jingle-Bell Rock • Merry Christmas, Darling • Rudolph the Red-Nosed Reindeer • Silver Bells.

VOL. 23 – SURF 00699635 / $14.95
Let's Go Trippin' • Out of Limits • Penetration • Pipeline • Surf City • Surfin' U.S.A. • Walk Don't Run • The Wedge.

VOL. 24 – ERIC CLAPTON 00699649 / $14.95
Badge • Bell Bottom Blues • Change the World • Cocaine • Key to the Highway • Lay Down Sally • White Room • Wonderful Tonight.

VOL. 25 – LENNON & McCARTNEY 00699642 / $14.95
Back in the U.S.S.R. • Drive My Car • Get Back • A Hard Day's Night • I Feel Fine • Paperback Writer • Revolution • Ticket to Ride.

VOL. 26 – ELVIS PRESLEY 00699643 / $14.95
All Shook Up • Blue Suede Shoes • Don't Be Cruel • Heartbreak Hotel • Hound Dog • Jailhouse Rock • Little Sister • Mystery Train.

VOL. 27 – DAVID LEE ROTH 00699645 / $14.95
Ain't Talkin' 'Bout Love • Dance the Night Away • Hot for Teacher • Just Like Paradise • A Lil' Ain't Enough • Runnin' with the Devil • Unchained • Yankee Rose.

VOL. 28 – GREG KOCH 00699646 / $14.95
Chief's Blues • Death of a Bassman • Dylan the Villain • The Grip • Holy Grail • Spank It • Tonus Diabolicus • Zoiks.

VOL. 29 – BOB SEGER 00699647 / $14.95
Against the Wind • Betty Lou's Gettin' Out Tonight • Hollywood Nights • Mainstreet • Night Moves • Old Time Rock & Roll • Rock and Roll Never Forgets • Still the Same.

VOL. 30 – KISS 00699644 / $14.95
Cold Gin • Detroit Rock City • Deuce • Firehouse • Heaven's on Fire • Love Gun • Rock and Roll All Nite • Shock Me.

VOL. 31 – CHRISTMAS HITS 00699652 / $14.95
Blue Christmas • Do You Hear What I Hear • Happy Holiday • I Saw Mommy Kissing Santa Claus • I'll Be Home for Christmas • Let It Snow! Let It Snow! Let It Snow! • Little Saint Nick • Snowfall.

VOL. 32 – THE OFFSPRING 00699653 / $14.95
Bad Habit • Come Out and Play • Gone Away • Gotta Get Away • Hit That • The Kids Aren't Alright • Pretty Fly (For a White Guy) • Self Esteem.

VOL. 33 – ACOUSTIC CLASSICS 00699656 / $14.95
Across the Universe • Babe, I'm Gonna Leave You • Crazy on You • Heart of Gold • Hotel California • I'd Love to Change the World • Thick As a Brick • Wanted Dead or Alive.

VOL. 34 – CLASSIC ROCK 00699658 / $14.95
Aqualung • Born to Be Wild • The Boys Are Back in Town • Brown Eyed Girl • Reeling in the Years • Rock'n Me • Rocky Mountain Way • Sweet Emotion.

VOL. 35 – HAIR METAL 00699660 / $14.95
Decadence Dance • Don't Treat Me Bad • Down Boys • Seventeen • Shake Me • Up All Night • Wait • Talk Dirty to Me.

VOL. 36 – SOUTHERN ROCK 00699661 / $14.95
Can't You See • Flirtin' with Disaster • Hold on Loosely • Jessica • Mississippi Queen • Ramblin' Man • Sweet Home Alabama • What's Your Name.

VOL. 37 – ACOUSTIC METAL 00699662 / $14.95
Every Rose Has Its Thorn • Fly to the Angels • Hole Hearted • Love Is on the Way • Love of a Lifetime • Signs • To Be with You • When the Children Cry.

VOL. 38 – BLUES 00699663 / $14.95
Boom Boom • Cold Shot • Crosscut Saw • Everyday I Have the Blues • Frosty • Further On up the Road • Killing Floor • Texas Flood.

VOL. 39 – '80S METAL 00699664 / $14.95
Bark at the Moon • Big City Nights • Breaking the Chains • Cult of Personality • Lay It Down • Living on a Prayer • Panama • Smokin' in the Boys Room.

VOL. 40 – INCUBUS 00699668 / $14.95
Are You In? • Drive • Megalomaniac • Nice to Know You • Pardon Me • Stellar • Talk Shows on Mute • Wish You Were Here.

VOL. 41 – ERIC CLAPTON 00699669 / $14.95
After Midnight • Can't Find My Way Home • Forever Man • I Shot the Sheriff • I'm Tore Down • Pretending • Running on Faith • Tears in Heaven.

VOL. 42 – CHART HITS 00699670 / $14.95
Are You Gonna Be My Girl • Heaven • Here Without You • I Believe in a Thing Called Love • Just Like You • Last Train Home • This Love • Until the Day I Die.

VOL. 43 – LYNYRD SKYNYRD 00699681 / $14.95
Don't Ask Me No Questions • Free Bird • Gimme Three Steps • I Know a Little • Saturday Night Special • Sweet Home Alabama • That Smell • You Got That Right.

VOL. 44 – JAZZ 00699689 / $14.95
I Remember You • I'll Remember April • Impressions • In a Mellow Tone • Moonlight in Vermont • On a Slow Boat to China • Things Ain't What They Used to Be • Yesterdays.

VOL. 46 – MAINSTREAM ROCK 00699722 / $14.95
Just a Girl • Keep Away • Kryptonite • Lightning Crashes • 1979 • One Step Closer • Scar Tissue • Torn.

VOL. 47 – HENDRIX SMASH HITS 00699723 / $16.95
All Along the Watchtower • Can You See Me? • Crosstown Traffic • Fire • Foxey Lady • Hey Joe • Manic Depression • Purple Haze • Red House • Remember • Stone Free • The Wind Cries Mary.

VOL. 48 – AEROSMITH CLASSICS 00699724 / $14.95
Back in the Saddle • Draw the Line • Dream On • Last Child • Mama Kin • Same Old Song & Dance • Sweet Emotion • Walk This Way.

VOL. 50 – NÜ METAL 00699726 / $14.95
Duality • Here to Stay • In the End • Judith • Nookie • So Cold • Toxicity • Whatever.

VOL. 51 – ALTERNATIVE '90S 00699727 / $14.95
Alive • Cherub Rock • Come As You Are • Give It Away • Jane Says • No Excuses • No Rain • Santeria.

VOL. 56 – FOO FIGHTERS 00699749 / $14.95
All My Life • Best of You • DOA • I'll Stick Around • Learn to Fly • Monkey Wrench • My Hero • This Is a Call.

VOL. 57 – SYSTEM OF A DOWN 00699751 / $14.95
Aerials • B.Y.O.B. • Chop Suey! • Innervision • Question! • Spiders • Sugar • Toxicity.

Prices, contents, and availability subject to change without notice.

FOR MORE INFORMATION, SEE YOUR LOCAL MUSIC DEALER, OR WRITE TO:

HAL·LEONARD® CORPORATION
7777 W. BLUEMOUND RD. P.O. BOX 13819 MILWAUKEE, WI 53213

Visit Hal Leonard online at www.halleonard.com

0106